Helping the Homeless
God's Word in Action

Duane Grady

BRETHREN PRESS
Elgin, Illinois

Helping the Homeless:
God's Word in Action

Copyright © 1988 by Duane Grady

BRETHREN PRESS, 1451 Dundee Avenue, Elgin, IL 60120

All rights reserved. No portion of this book may be reproduced in any form or by any process or technique without the written consent of the publisher, except for brief quotations embodied in critical articles or reviews.

Cover design by Kathy Kline Miller
Cover photo by Phil Grout

Grateful acknowledgment is made to Lauree Hersch Meyer, Myra Herr, and Karen Harlander for their help in preparing the manuscript, and to the Board of Directors, Interfaith Council for the Homeless, Chicago, Illinois, for their support of this project. Special appreciation is expressed to Board President, Bishop Sherman G. Hicks, for his skillful leadership.

Scripture quotations are from the Revised Standard Version of the Bible, copyrighted 1946, 1952, 1971, 1973, 1977 by the National Council of Churches of Christ in the U.S.A., Division of Education and Ministry.

Library of Congress Cataloging in Publication Data
Grady, Duane.
    Helping the homeless: God's word in action/Duane Grady.
      p.   cm.
    Bibliography: p.
    ISBN 0-87178-349-5
    1. Church work with the homeless—United States. 2. Homelessness—United States. 3. Homelessness—Religious aspects—Christianity.
    I. Title.
BV4456.G7 1988
261.8'325—dc19   88-21696
                                                                                   CIP

Manufactured in the United States of America

Contents

Introduction v
1. Creation and Community 1
2. The Family of God 7
3. Fulfilling God's Covenant 13
4. Worship and Redemption 19
5. Reaching Out 25
6. Dreams and Vision......................... 31
7. Destruction and Rebuilding 37
8. Joy and Celebration 45
9. Changing Priorities....................... 51
Appendix A Causes of Homelessness 57
Appendix B Worship Resources 61
Appendix C God's Word in Action 79
Appendix D Resources 81
Epilogue..................................... 85

*This book is dedicated to my children,
Jacob and Anna, in the hope that they
will live in a world without homelessness
and to Bev whose love and support has given
me a family and a home.*

Introduction

Seven years ago, I began to work directly with homeless persons. In reviewing the work of these seven years, I am reminded of the story of Jacob and Rachel in Genesis 29:15–30. Jacob fell in love with Rachel and contracted to work for her father, Leban, who agreed that after seven years, Jacob and Rachel could marry. Jacob willingly fulfilled his part of the bargain only to be tricked by Leban. Jacob secretly was given Rachel's older sister, Leah, as a wife. Without doubt, Jacob felt deceived. His seven years of labor had not produced the results that he had intended. He was required to work an additional seven years before Rachel could become his wife.

When I reflect upon my last seven years, I share in Jacob's disappointment. I, too, expected my work, and that of the thousands like me, would produce different results. During the 1980s, significant attention has been paid to the problem of homelessness. Exciting programs have emerged. Yet, homelessness has grown steadily worse. While I do not believe our efforts have been in vain, I am bitterly disappointed that the harsh realities of homelessness which I have seen all too often, will entrap even more men, women, families, youth, and children. I have no doubt that this is a problem which will require serious attention in the years ahead.

Homelessness is a long-term problem in the United States. It will require persons and institutions of vision, strength, and resilience. For Christians, it will be necessary to study the Bible diligently and to let God guide us in pursuing concrete steps toward alleviating the crisis of homelessness.

No one can deny that this topic is difficult to address. As we carefully read and strive to discern the scriptures highlighted here, let us remember that the Bible promises good things to those who are oppressed and to those who are faithful. We can rely upon this hope because the Bible continually reminds us that we are not alone in the world and we are aided and sustained by more power than we can imagine. Let us go forth then to love and serve God with gladness.

We will be aided in this work by remembering that homelessness is a condition familiar to God's people. There are numerous occasions related in the Bible when the people of God have experienced homelessness. The first four chapters of Genesis tell two stories. Adam and Eve are expelled from humanity's first home in the Garden to live in the wilderness and Cain is sentenced to a life of wandering (to have no home) as punishment for killing his brother. But, even in these stories, God makes the point that new life is possible through the children of Adam and Eve. Cain, although a murderer, will always bear the protective mark of God; thus, Cain is never forsaken by God.

A definition of homelessness has kept social scientists and researchers busy in recent years. From a biblical perspective, homelessness is a state in which a person or group lives without direct access to food, shelter, clothing, and emotional stability. Homelessness is both an economic condition and a status within a community.

Biblical tradition includes a wealth of stories about God's People being led or forced into conditions of homelessness. To highlight just a few:

1. Abraham is called to leave his country, his family, and his father's house to pursue the promised land (Gen. 12:1-2).
2. Moses leads Israel into the wilderness from Egypt for forty years of wandering (Exod. 13:17-22 ff).
3. Ruth leaves her people to join Naomi in Judah (Ruth 1:1-22).
4. In fear of his life, David flees into the wilderness to avoid Saul's threats of death (1 Sam. 22:1 ff).
5. Israel is repeatedly invaded and its people made captives (see Psalm 137, Lamentations, Jeremiah, and Isaiah).
6. Fleeing Herod's paranoia, Joseph and Mary steal away to Egypt with the infant Jesus, leaving their home and livelihood behind (Matt. 2:13-18).

7. Jesus tells a would-be disciple that "Foxes have holes and the birds of the air have nests, but the Son of Man has nowhere to lay his head." (Luke 9:58)

The Bible consistently emphasizes that God is with the people even as they experience trauma and homelessness. Ours is a God who lives and breathes and suffers with all of us.

In our world, we need to have the faith and the courage to see our homeless neighbors. This Bible Study guide offers scriptural insights into this current problem. As we look at Jesus' relationship with others and his ethics, we are reminded that God calls us and the Church to a variety of responses. One option, however, cannot be found among the faithful in scripture—to choose indifference and ignorance.

Ours is a God who cares and who responds. As Easter people, we are called to participate in God's Kingdom as it has been announced by Christ and as it points toward the finality of God's reign.

Jesus has taught us how to live and how to pray. The New Testament urges us to honor God and to desire "God's Kingdom, on earth as it is in heaven." Because we believe these words, we will direct our attention to those around us. Although homelessness is just one issue we are called to address, it is a concern that as Christians our heritage and our God calls us to make a priority as we strive to live as disciples of Christ.

The written materials for each session have purposely been kept to a minimum. A suggestion for structuring the sessions is to encourage persons to read both the scriptures and commentary prior to each session. Sessions can begin with reading the scriptures aloud and a summary of the commentary and case study. Considerable time for discussion and questions should be scheduled.

Duane Grady
Chicago, Illinois

Creation and Community

1

All persons are children of God and worthy of our love and respect.

Purpose: As Christians, consider what it means to view persons who are homeless as equal participants in God's creation and as persons whom God expects us to love.

Genesis 1:26, 27, 32; Leviticus 19:18; Deuteronomy 6:5; Luke 16:19–31; James 2:1–4, 8–9

The creation story emphasizes that God is the creator of life and that this creation is "very good." Human beings are created in the likeness of God and are brought into covenant with God. Human life is not blessed and declared good on its own merits or accomplishments but rather, God affirms the value and worth of life in and of itself. Persons are special because God has made them. God's protection is available to all human life.

Within the Judeo-Christian heritage, two understandings play a critical role in defining the religious view of the world. First, God is known to be the ultimate expression of our devotion. God is seen as the source of creation and the sustainer of all life. There is no other god. Second, we are to love our neighbors as we love ourselves. This requires that we see worth in others and recognize that all persons are equally important in God's eyes. The purpose of this tenet is not to lower our consideration of ourselves, but to uplift the importance of other persons whom we are to see as our neighbors.

When we recognize that there is only one God, then all of humanity is subject to and deserving of God's blessings. God is Sovereign, and all of God's creation belongs to one family. As a consequence, then, it follows that all persons are our neighbors. If God does not divide the human race, then we ought not ignore or deny the needs of others. God is One, and we are one people. As God's children, we are called to love everyone and to consider the needs of others as important as our own.

In both the Leviticus and Deuteronomy passages, the sense of the word love is emotional affiliation. True love must be felt. It cannot be legalized or demanded. Deuteronomy speaks of love in the same way that a person cares for immediate family. Love in Deuteronomy has a dual purpose; to remind us that our relationship with God must be an intimate one and to shape a sincere expression of caring for others in us. Loving others is meant to be an act of obedience to God.

We have seen from looking at human history and at our own social practices that people are often divided into groups and classes. These distinctions are not divinely inspired. Every attempt to categorize people must begin with the assumption that some persons are worth more than others. God's good creation is only affirmed when we recognize the special importance of one another.

The writer of James encourages us to look at more than a person's outer appearance. In God's family, a person's clothing or economic status should not separate one from the worshiping community. There is more to a person's character than outward appearance. As God looks into the hearts and minds of each of us, we also should look for the true nature in all people we meet. God has given us life and invites us to live with others, respectful of that good gift which has also been given to them.

The story of Lazarus tells us that acceptance into God's kingdom is not based on a person's wealth or worldly accomplishments. Poverty is not a sign of God's disfavor. Lazarus enters heaven; the rich man does not. For what reason were these eternal assignments made? We must assume that Lazarus was judged worthy and faithful. And the rich man?

Based on the story as recorded, the only clue is that he is rejected for the sin of ignoring his brother Lazarus. However, the rich man did not ignore Lazarus totally. But the scraps that fell from his table did not meet the expectations of God. The idea that Lazarus, as a poor beggar, could enter heaven was radical in Jesus' day.

Two thousand years ago, the belief that wealth gave proof to God's blessings was popular. Lazarus, even though a poor man, is asked to be the message bearer to the rich man's family to warn them. In today's world, the poor have a message we ought to hear. Might not Jesus be hearing the voices of Lazarus' of today?

An important element of the Lazarus story is the chasm separating Lazarus from the rich man. Following their deaths, the distance between them is so great that it is impossible for this barrier to be crossed. Similarly, in their living, a great gulf divided the men but this was a separation that could have been overcome. The story calls us to recognize those we might see as different from ourselves in lifestyle, economics, and beliefs and to build bridges across those differences.

Too often, the homeless are seen as different from the rest of society because we focus on specific problems common to those who are homeless and regard them as unique only to that community.

For example, the homeless are frequently stereotyped as alcoholics. While this problem certainly exists among those who are homeless, this is not the only group to experience alcoholism. A study of the rates of alcoholism in the United States will show that the two social classes with the highest percentages of alcohol abuse are the very poor and the very wealthy. Alcoholism is not just a poor person's disease. It cuts across social and economic boundaries.

Likewise, many of the problems that the homeless encounter are familiar to those of other social classes. Who among us has not felt afraid or alone? Who among us has not felt limited or ignored? If we take the time to truly talk with persons who are homeless, we will find that they have many of the same needs, ideas, dreams, and experiences as persons who are not homeless.

The challenge for the faith community is our response to the homeless. Will we too emphasize our differences or will we work to find ways to include the homeless in our worship and communal life? This question can be answered best as we read God's word and strive to be faithful to it in the midst of a world which offers alternative values—a world which is too often divisive and hostile. The community of faith has been given the message of shalom and reconciliation.

Russ's Story

Russ was a regular guest at an emergency overnight shelter in the basement of a Lutheran Church. He was well-known and well-liked by the shelter staff and volunteers. On several occasions, Russ was asked to participate in the morning worship service, but he always declined. Finally, he was asked why he did not wish to come to the worship service. Russ was willing to admit that he was afraid that his clothes would not be suitable for attending worship.

Russ was assured that his clothing would be fine. So, finally, he agreed to attend the next service. He sat near the back and noticed that no one sat on the bench with him, although several persons greeted him in a friendly manner. He was glad that he recognized several volunteers from the shelter and he enjoyed talking to them after the service. He did, however, notice that three people leered at him. He overheard them say to each other, "I knew that if we allowed that shelter to be downstairs, some of them would filter in outside of the shelter hours. He probably only wants a handout."

From this conversation, Russ understood that he was not really welcomed by the congregation. He was different. That night, he decided not to return to the church shelter and went instead to a shelter run by the city.

Discussion Questions

1. How would your congregation act if a homeless person came to worship?

2. When you see homeless persons, either on TV or on the streets, what do you most notice about them? Do you think of them as just like us or do you think of them as different?
3. In what ways are each of us homeless? Explain.

Additional texts: Proverbs 29:13; Luke 10:25-28

The Family of God

2

As God's children we are called to see ourselves in others.

Purpose: To help Christians identify the common bond between their experiences in faith and the trials faced by the homeless.

Exodus 13:17-22; 14:11-13; 23:9; Deuteronomy 10:17-22; John 15:1-17; Matthew 7:12

To the Israelite people, the Exodus experience was remembered as a time when God led them from slavery into the wilderness. The wilderness experience itself was a period of testing and development as well as uncertainty and homelessness. Prior to the Exodus, Israel had no home. In Egypt they were slaves, forced against their will to accept a lifestyle that was hard and unfulfilling. During the wilderness experience, which lasted 40 years, Israel learned to trust God and to wait in anticipation of God's saving actions. The people were transformed from a slave people into a community able to live under the Law of Moses.

Almost immediately on entering the wilderness, the people began to question God's leadership. Repeatedly, they feared for their safety and anguished over where to find food, their lack of water, and the continual need for shelter.

They turned in anger against Moses and even began to look back more favorably on their lives in Egypt as slaves.

This yearning for the pain of slavery points out the difficult nature of the wilderness experience. Moses led Israel into a difficult life-threatening situation, not unlike that faced by the homeless of our time.

The wilderness experience is remembered each year in Judaism in an observation of the Seder meal and during the Sukkoth observation, at which time Jews reside in temporary dwellings that provide minimal shelter as a reminder that there continues to be people who live without secure shelter. The Seder meal is also an opportunity to remember the poor and the homeless. Many biblical scholars believe that Jesus' last supper with the disciples was the Seder meal.

Most Christian groups in the United States include a wilderness type experience as part of their heritage. During the past 300 years, millions of Christians fled their homelands in search of new beginnings. Once in the United States, westward migrations continued the pattern of upheaval and drastic change.

How are we to utilize these experiences in considering our homeless neighbors? Deuteronomy 10:17-22 commits us to see ourselves in others. We are called to remember the stranger because we too were once strangers in a strange land. In our religious identification with Israel's wilderness experience, we can understand it to be a resembling the life of many homeless people today. We can also look at our personal lives and remember periods when we felt alone, afraid, and without security. These experiences ought to bring us closer to the homeless who feel these same emotions. We need not attempt to experience homelessness in order to empathize with the homeless.

We can point beyond the wilderness experience. Israel did not remain in the desert forever. God's promises to Abraham (Gen. chapters 12-15) were fulfilled. It remains the task of God's people to announce the Good News to the homeless—Good News that includes the joy of a place to call home. We can provide signs of active hope and help God in the task of leading today's homeless out of the slavery of living without adequate shelter.

Jesus' words in John 15:1-17, remind us that we are obliged to love others because God has first loved us. Our relationship with others is symbolized by the image of the vine. We, as children of God, are connected to one another and we draw our strength from the same life giving source.

The commission to love one another is similar to Jesus' ethic of the Golden Rule, "Do unto others as you would have them do unto you." (Matt. 7:12). If we are to live the Golden Rule, it is necessary that we think about other people and how our behavior affects them.

Using the scriptures noted previously, it is important to stress that as Christians, we need to respond to the homeless with compassion. We should be aware of the similarities between their struggles and our lives of faith.

Imagine yourself homeless or, perhaps, as a family recently evicted from your home. How would you want others to see you? What help might you need? Thinking about the kind of treatment we would want will guide us in helping others.

You may not be able to imagine yourself homeless. Twenty years ago, few people have imagined established farmers in Iowa or Kansas facing bankruptcy and the loss of fourth generation family farms. A frequent statement heard from today's homeless is, "I never imagined this could happen to me."

A temptation in reviewing our lives is to see our experiences and opportunities as unique. While it is exciting to believe that what we experience is a new revelation, the biblical tradition will remind us that we are a part of an ongoing story. Formed by our heritage, we can, in turn, be a living testimony of God's Word. As participants in a larger story, we are able to connect what has happened to us with what happens to other persons. This understanding makes it possible for us to identify with the experiences of the homeless.

Living in the tradition of fallen humanity, we experience homelessness as alienation from God and from one another. Christians look forward to a time when they are no longer alienated, but it is understood that this can only happen through God's saving grace. We, like the homeless, are dependent on resources which we do not fully control. The vulnerability of the homeless is a condition with which we can identify as part of our lives of faith. Let us wait together, faithful to the commandment, "Love one another as I have loved you."

Mike's Story

Mike is a frequent guest of an overnight shelter. Before he became homeless, Mike worked for twelve years in a steel mill. In 1979, the steel mill began laying off its workers and it was closed completely three years later. Mike and his coworkers were without work for the first time in their lives.

Growing up near the steel mill, Mike had planned to work there until he reached retirement age. Since he had been a steel worker for twelve years, he looked for similar employment.

With so many others looking for work, Mike found jobs hard to find. His unemployment checks were larger than most part-time and minimum wage jobs, so he did not take those. He did not realize how quickly the unemployment compensation would run out.

Mike is self-assertive and confident. So, when he could no longer pay his monthly rent, he moved into an overnight shelter, expecting to have a short tenure there. He learned quickly how difficult it is to find employment without a phone number or permanent address. Potential employers were not sympathetic to his situation. Maintaining a clean appearance without daily access to showers and clean clothes was even more difficult.

Mike heard from others at the overnight shelter that he could sell newspapers on the street to earn money. Each morning, awakened by shelter staff at 4:00 a.m., Mike walks eight blocks to stand in line for the newspaper selling jobs. Normally he has the opportunity to work from 5:30 a.m. to 10:30 a.m. selling papers at a busy street corner. Some mornings it is cold, other times it is raining. Mike looks for this job each day for an average pay of $8.00.

After working, Mike walks the mile to a soup kitchen for lunch where the food is good but limited to only one serving per person. Toward the end of each month, the line becomes longer. Mike spends the rest of his day walking or at a drop-in center for street people. He thinks of creative ways to spend his wages. Twice each month, he saves three days' wages and splurges by getting a room at a nearby Single Room Occupancy Hotel.

At 10 p.m. each night, Mike returns to the overnight shelter to rest before returning to his newspaper selling job. His dreams of working again in the abandoned steel mill seem harder to him than the mat and floor he sleeps on each evening. Mike sees little hope for his future.

Discussion questions

1. Imagine what it would be like for you to be homeless. Share your concerns.
2. Think about a time when you experienced being in a wilderness. What happened for things to get better?
3. What do you believe to be the primary cause of homelessness?
4. What do you have in common with persons who are homeless? How does your life differ from the stories in this study guide?
5. How do you feel God sees homeless persons? What biblical passages come to mind?

Fulfilling God's Covenant 3

The poor are a sign of the failure of God's People to obey the covenant.

Purpose: To understand that the tragedy of homelessness is an example of how the religious community does not fulfill its obligations to live as a just society.

Deuteronomy 15:4-7; Amos 4:1-3; 5:7-13; Jeremiah 5:20-31; Luke 12:13-21; Acts 2:42-47

One of the remarkable features of Israelite law, especially emphasized in Deuteronomy, is the deep concern for the welfare of all individuals within the community. A primary purpose of the institutions of government and the economy was to ensure that the needs of all persons were met, especially the needs of the weak. Within this tradition it was understood that the protection of all persons had a direct relationship to the well-being of the community itself.

As stated in Deuteronomy, it was impossible for a society to be blessed by God unless it cared for the poor. The injunction, "Let there be no poor among you," is a command without exceptions. The reward for caring for the poor is to receive a recognition that all persons are created in the same image of God and that no persons can be regarded as less than human.

The reference to the cancellation of all debts after seven years is a recognition that Israel has not yet truly obeyed God.

If there were true obedience, then there would be no poor and hence no need for this regulation. This passage is harshly critical of any political, religious, or economic philosophy that justifies poverty or that fails to see the poor as a sign of unfaithfulness.

The prophetic writings are well known for their resounding social criticisms, especially against the treatment given the poor. Amos uses strong language to express God's disgust with the ill treatment that the poor receive. Amos announced to a nation which had a very wealthy class of people that the security they felt in military victory and accumulated riches would not protect them from God's wrath. In some of the Bible's most colorful language, Amos labeled the wealthy women of Samaria as *cows* because they demanded that their husbands increase their wealth and he condemned them for seeking their own pleasure while others suffered.

The social criticism of Amos is not merely an attack on materialism; Amos saw that part of God's community suffers due to the selfishness expressed by the wealthy. Amos was able to discern an economic system that is unfairly weighted against the poor and that the poor do not exist because of their own failures. The poor exist because God's justice has been distorted and perverted.

Jeremiah also strongly places into focus the economics of God versus human selfishness. Because God intended that there be no poverty in our bountiful creation, the measure of any society is how it responds to those persons with needs. Jeremiah saw among his own people both wealth and poverty. Yet, he knew that the wealth could not be appreciated because, as we have seen in Deuteronomy, such things are often obtained by ignoring the covenant commands to help the poor. Wealth that is maintained in the face of poverty is illegitimate. Jeremiah pronounces God's judgement upon the people who do not make a priority of the need to help the poor, and he is especially critical of the prophets who remain silent on this sin or who seem comfortable living with it. The truth, as Jeremiah boldly proclaims, is that a people who accept poverty cannot be a people of God and that the joys experienced by those who are comfortable while others suffer are only temporary.

Within the Christian tradition, the hoarding of possessions has been placed into the context of a failure to trust God. Jesus states (Luke 16:13 and Mark 10:25) that there exists a conflict between obedience to God and attachment to money. It is probable that Jesus had the Deuteronomic economic code in mind in telling the parable of the rich man and the harvest. The theme again reminds us that a desire to care only for one's own needs places us outside the community where God's law is practiced and lived.

In the early Christian community, all possessions were owned in common. Here, no one went hungry and it can be assumed that food was shared with persons outside the community. In such a community, poverty is frequently an unknown factor.

The implications for us in these readings are deep. In contrast, we often hear the philosophy "God helps those who help themselves," which argues that the poor are responsible for their condition. Such arguments cannot stand alongside the biblical view that reducing poverty is a religious community's obligation. This philosophy also fails to understand that the strength of a community is dependent upon the well-being of all its members.

As we look at our cities, we see much of what Amos and Jeremiah saw. We can see impressive buildings and cultural riches. We can also see thousands and thousands of homeless persons. A biblical perspective forces us to acknowledge both realities and to understand that our acceptance of poverty will not win us God's favor.

In recent years, new and modern housing units have been constructed in the downtown areas of many of our nation's cities. This construction has begun to change many areas from a community of low income housing to an area of luxury apartments. While there are some who rejoice in this *improvement* of the economic base for the neighborhood, a biblical people must remember that this new construction results in the destruction of older, low income housing units. In many instances, Single Room Occupancy hotels (SROs) and low income apartment buildings where some residents had lived for many years are being torn down.

The loss of SRO units in many cities is a result of conversion and redevelopment rather than decline and abandonment. In Chicago, SROs have been replaced by office buildings, even though commercial office space has a vacancy rate of 17.3 percent. During a five year period (1979-1984), the construction of luxury housing increased 500 percent while during the same period at least 5,000 SRO units were lost. During the late 1970s, New York City's SRO stock dropped from 50,000 to 19,619. San Francisco lost 10,000 SROs. From 1978-1983 Philadelphia lost 26 percent of its available low income housing units. Virtually none of these lost units have been replaced, resulting in the scarcity of housing for the very poor.

Housing news for families is also bleak. Public housing projects are overcrowded and falling into disrepair as the federal government reduced spending by 75 percent from 1981-87. Indianapolis has lost 30 percent of its public housing units during the 1980s. Baltimore has 13,000 families vying for 17,000 available units. In Jersey City, families are placed on a 10 year waiting list where public housing has a 115 percent occupancy rate due to overcrowding and a 1 percent turn over rate.

Construction of office buildings and luxury apartments have been aided by government loans, tax breaks, and other public subsidies. This economic viewpoint not only ignores free market principles, but also places potential profits over the need for low income housing.

What happens to low income individuals and families during this transition? Studies have shown that in many cases they are left homeless. One of the primary causes of this homelessness is that the same income which had provided sufficiently for them to have housing is no longer adequate. We have seen clearly that the loss of low income housing units is a major cause of homelessness.

Marilyn's Story

Marilyn was a long term resident in a single room occupancy hotel in Atlanta. She had lived there since the death of her husband ten years ago. Because she was a long term resident and paid for her room by the month, Marilyn's rent was less than other residents who paid by the week.

Approximately one-half of the hotel's occupants had lived there for more than three years. Marilyn had made many friends among the other hotel residents. Her neighbors and friends looked out for her. They did things for her like going out to get her medicine during cold weather.

One day a sign appeared in the hotel lobby announcing that a community renovation project was going to be built and that the hotel was going to be closed. The notice appeared on February 3, and the residents were told that they would need to move by the end of the month.

Marilyn could not locate another room at the same rate she had been spending for her housing. At the end of the month she learned from some other hotel residents that she could stay at an emergency overnight shelter, but there was no place to store her possessions. The shelter was only open from 10:00 p.m. until 6:00 a.m. and only during the colder months, November through March. At the end of March, she would again need to find another place to stay.

Marilyn's fixed monthly income is $160.00. The least expensive hotel room she could find was $180.00 per month. Her only other option is to try to sell her food stamps (she receives $80.00 per month) and use this money to rent a room in another SRO—although she will need also to find a way to eat and pay for her medication.

Discussion Questions

1. If you were Marilyn, what would you do?
2. What do you see as the cause of poverty?
3. How do we act in the face of poverty? Do we:
   a) tolerate it?
   b) ignore it?
   c) hope it will go away?
   d) blame the poor for the condition they are in?
4. How can we work actively to reform our governmental systems in order actually to reduce poverty?
5. Homelessness is a complicated problem that no one of us can solve alone. How can we work together to bring about change?

Worship and Redemption 4

Service to others is a function of worship.

Purpose: To understand that worship necessitates considering the needs of other persons.

Exodus 20:1-17; Isaiah 1:10-17; Matthew 5:24; 1 Corinthians 11:17-34

The Bible frequently speaks to the temptation of worshiping false gods. Idolatry is the sin of representing God falsely, attributing characteristics to God that are not true, or worshiping something that is not God. Idolatry occurs in two ways: 1) The denial of God's transcendent and living nature by worshiping God as a graven image. Any graven image is an attempt to define and control God. The Bible strongly forbids this activity (Exod. 32:1-10). 2) The adoption of forms of worship that distort or conceal who God is. This occurs when believers profess to follow God but do not follow God's Word. For example, many heretical beliefs have been practiced. These beliefs, however, do not have the God of the Bible at their center.

The ten Commandments provide guidance in shaping our relationship with God and with our neighbors. The prohibition against making God into a graven image acknowledges that we can easily be tempted into serving other gods. Having no other gods before Yahweh means questioning the priorities in our lives. This commandment forces us to examine the things which are truly most important to us.

God's jealousy as noted in Exod. 20:5 holds us accountable for the priorities we make for our time, our resources, and our thoughts. God is aware that our world tempts us to trust and to serve "as gods" such values as career goals, money, freedom, and human relationships. But, these gods will disillusion us. They are only substitutes for the life-sustaining God of the Bible.

Following the commandments that define our relationship with God are six statements affecting communal life. The ten Commandments unite the reciprocal responsibilities of worshiping God and respecting other persons. These attitudes if put into practice together form the basis for a life of faithfulness.

The prohibition against representing God as a graven image also applies to what God has made. We have seen that human beings are created by God in God's own image. It is idolatrous to label or falsely identify God or God's creation. When we discuss homelessness, we are obligated to avoid labels such as bum, alcoholic, street person, or bag lady. These terms cannot adequately or justly portray a person as God has made them or as God sees them. Terms like homeless person only serve to describe a condition, not a person. God calls us to see one another as brothers and sisters with whom we share a common heritage.

Isaiah 1:10-17 speaks to the problem of worship. This scripture along with Amos 5:21-24; Hosea 6:6, 8:11-14; and Micah 6:6-8, boldly states that worshiping God requires more than ritual motions. The prophets were keenly aware of the problem of hypocrisy. Offerings which are made without sincere repentance lose their religious meaning. Ours is a God of action who desires our sincere devotion. Sincerity by its very nature cannot be faked—it must be honestly felt. Worship, then, is aimed to help believers to prepare their hearts for acting justly.

Worship for the prophetic writers required examining our relationships with others. God is concerned with our behavior toward other persons, especially the weak and the vulnerable. Worship must always include expressions of morality. Isaiah tells us that God hates worship that is insincere and worship that ignores human suffering. In today's world, if we try to worship God without remembering the homeless, we have not understood the nature of worship. Isaiah argues that God will not hear these prayers.

The passage in Isaiah is rich in imagery. The reference to Gomorrah points to the foremost symbol of evil in the Old Testament and forcefully tells us that worship without justice is evil. Isaiah describes a person praying with hands outstretched. If a person is worshiping God, the hands will be open and in a posture to share. If not, the person's hands are grasping for personal gain or are used as a shield from God. These hands are bloody from the crime of selfishness which God abhors.

The language of Isaiah is direct and confrontational. Its brashness indicates impatience in the knowledge that people are suffering. Human suffering is always an urgent matter. Isaiah saw this suffering at the same time he saw the religious institutions and leaders of his time failing to incorporate these problems into their worship activities. To this contradiction, he was not silent.

Jesus also speaks to the connection between worship and our relationships with others. Matthew 5:24 states that it is impossible to worship if we harbor anger or alienation toward others. Jesus does not leave any room for avoiding the action of reconciliation. He commands reconciliation.

The gift at the altar here is reminiscent of the sacificial offering in Isaiah. Surely, Jesus who calls us to see all persons as neighbors tells us today that we must first be reconciled with the homeless if we desire to worship. This reconciliation will require that we recognize the existence of the homeless around us and that we learn to know them and to understand their problems. We cannot be reconciled with persons whom we do not know. Finally, we will need to worship with them in ways that introduce solutions to their plight.

Christian worship seeks to unite prophetic vision with redeeming grace. It is important to know that God loves us if we are to love others, but accepting God's love will compel us into sharing this gift beyond ourselves. A theology of the cross will remember Christ's suffering and resurrection. To emphasize prophetic vision at the exclusion of redemptive grace distorts Christian worship just as seeking salvation without praying for the needs of others will bring the criticism voiced by both Jesus and Isaiah.

If there is any doubt that Christians must be attentive to how they worship God, Paul removes it in his letter to the Corinthians. From his letter, we learn that the people of Corinth were attempting to celebrate the Lord's Supper together. But, Paul admonishes them in the same spirit as Isaiah for performing this task as a ritual and not as the bonding encounter taught by Christ. Paul was angered with the separate factions within the fellowship and by how the poor were made to feel. Sensitive to the way in which persons of lesser financial means were treated, he rebukes the congregation for causing them embarrassment.

Paul argues that concern for others was lacking in the celebration of this meal. He states firmly that the behavior of the wealthy towards the poor prevented the meal from being the Lord's Supper. According to Paul, this behavior showed the absence of the spirit of Christ within the congregation. He directs them to change their attitude.

Martha's Encounter

It was two weeks before Christmas and Martha, a lawyer recently admitted to the bar, decided to visit the church in her neighborhood. Although, it had been several years since she had entered a church, she had attended services faithfully with her family before leaving home for college. She had almost forgotten why she stopped going, then remembered the long nights of studying in law school. At that time, she had decided that going to church really was not necessary if a person continued to pray. She also had rationalized, "I will hurt my health if I do not get more sleep and taking care of one's health is a Christian behavior."

Martha entered the church and took a seat in the rear of the sanctuary. Christmas music brought back pleasant memories and she was glad she had come. When the offering plate was passed—she put in $5.00.

It was not long into the sermon that her mood suddenly changed. Rather than the comforting stories about Christmas trees that she had heard as a child, the minister used his sermon to talk about the homeless. He mentioned that the baby Jesus had become homeless in the flight to Egypt and that it was the persecution of joblessness that caused many people to be homeless today.

The minister read from Matthew 25:31–46 to illustrate that the Christian community is obligated to help homeless people. True Christianity does not allow this problem to exist, he announced. The sermon ended with a plea for persons to make a Christmas gift of volunteer time to a neighborhood shelter. The words Martha heard and understood most clearly was that volunteering time was more important that donating money.

Throughout the rest of the day, Martha felt uneasy. She had ventured back to church because it was Christmastime and she wanted to experience more of a holiday spirit. She had not anticipated a lecture on social responsibility.

Martha experienced tension all week. There were her anxieties brought about by her recent church attendance. She remembered, as well, her grandmother telling of the Great Depression when men frequently knocked on the door asking for food. Martha's grandmother always cheerfully told her how good it felt to share with others who had so little.

By the end of the week, Martha decided to telephone the minister to talk more about her feelings. Beginning the conversation by expressing her disappointment that a social problem had been highlighted during the Christmas season, she asked, "I have no problem with the churches responding to social issues, but couldn't you have found a better time?"

"Unfortunately, I cannot agree with you," responded the minister. "Christmas is about God's gift to us. Because God has given so much to us, we need to share with others."

Martha paused, and then revealed what was really troubling here. "Look, perhaps you are right. But so many of the poor are that way because of their own bad choices. Isn't it true that God helps those who help themselves?" she asked.

"Not if God's word is obeyed," answered the minister, "and I don't think that you would have that opinion if you learned to know some homeless people. Their situation is much more complex."

"I guess what bothers me is that you sound as if I should have already done that," she responded. "I have never even seen a homeless person, let alone learned to know one. I cannot be responsible for something I know nothing about."

The minister breathed slowly then answered, "It is hard for me to believe you can live in this neighborhood and not see homeless people. Perhaps you saw but did not focus your attention. Do you ever watch TV? There have been a number of recent programs about homelessness."

"When I get home from work, I need to relax. I guess those types of programs have been on but I quickly changed channels," Martha admitted. "Are you telling me it is my fault for needing entertainment?"

"Let me say this," began the minister, "The human family includes many people. We all need one another and we are wrong to assume that our lives can be fulfilling if we do not learn to know persons from other cultures or from different social classes. I believe God has planted a seed of knowledge in your heart. Your task is to let it grow."

"But why do I feel so lousy if giving is supposed to make a person feel good," Martha wondered. "What have you given to the homeless?" the minister asked. "Well, nothing yet," she responded.

"Then, you have answered your own question. What if I give you the telephone number of the local shelter," asked the minister. "And, please do not expect your reward to come quickly. Growth takes time."

Discussion Questions

1. What was Martha's worship experience? God touched Martha in a way she did not expect. Has this ever happened to you?
2. How do you define worship?
3. Have you ever volunteered time with homeless people? How did you feel about this experience?
4. What words would you use to describe a homeless person?
5. Discuss ways your congregation might reach out to the homeless?

Reaching Out

5

God requires that we be charitable with our resources and give to others.

Purpose: To understand the need to use our resources for the benefit of all.

Deuteronomy 15:7-11; Isaiah 58:1-12; Luke 18:18-23; 1 John 3:17

Because we have failed to fulfill God's covenant, there are poor among us. Our desire to fulfill the covenant drives us to work even harder to create a society where persons do not need to sleep in alleys and to eat out of garbage cans. One way to recognize our responsibilities as the people of God is by sharing our resources with those in need. We can work together to find long-term solutions to the problems of homelessness and hunger.

The Deuteronomic texts set forth some important criteria for giving to others. We recognize the needs of others by remembering that we too have needs. We must give thanks to God for what we have. Justice is a work of God and even if we forget the orphan and the widow, the Bible reminds us that God does not. When we look upon the faces of the hungry, we are seeing children of God who are members of our human family.

Our giving is to be without resentment and without hardening our hearts. We are to give to others with open hands and without determining their worthiness. We give because God had commanded it and this commandment holds fast even when persons justify selfishness by arguing that it really does no good to share with others. God does not ask that we look for results or that we help only those in whom we can see progress being made.

The Isaiah scripture points out the distinction between genuine worship and ritualized motions. Isaiah criticizes worship that ignores the needs of others, especially those who are hungry and homeless. Ours is a God of action and a God who calls us to share with others freely and lovingly.

The progress toward giving freely and openly is a spiritual journey. We cannot hide our true feelings from God. Even if we give with worldly flair, God can see our true motivation. God when we give with resentment is aware. Thus, we have violated the Deuteronomic Covenant.

When we consider the needs of others honestly, we can see that there are some persons who will always require our assistance. The biblical images of the widow and the orphan are examples of persons who depend on the generosity of others. In that society, even young and able widows could not work. Because they could no longer depend on their husbands, they turned to the religious community. In every society, there are persons who will not be able to provide their own livelihood.

Among the homeless, a significant percentage are persons with real emotional or physical limitations. During the 1970s, the policy of deinstitutionalization was begun. The initial intent of this effort was to release persons with less severe emotional difficulties from institutions. This policy was made feasible as new drug treatments advanced mental health care. However, adequate community services were not developed to aid these persons in their efforts at independent living. Literally, thousands of individuals were released from mental instutitions with very limited skills in living outside of an institutional setting. As a result, many of these persons, left on their own, have ended up on the streets. They have added to the number of emotionally ill persons who are homeless.

For any homeless person, living on the streets is an emotionally draining experience. The high level of stress often begins to undermine more and more of a person's self-confidence. Under these kinds of pressures, emotional illness can develop and certainly will grow worse in a person who has a previous history of emotional distress.

Obviously, emergency shelters are not solutions for the mentally and physically handicapped. Yet, until new programs are provided to help these people, the emergency shelter network remains their only source of protection from street violence.

Acts of charity are both commitments of love and strides toward justice. If we love other persons, we will help them. But in order to help them we must first recognize their presence and their needs. The attempt to argue that we have not seen persons in need cannot release us from our responsibility to be charitable. God holds us accountable to seek out persons who need our assistance and to help them. A failure to do so reflects our distance from God and from the Covenant. In other words, as we make more room for God in our hearts, we will respond more quickly to those who need our help.

As our relationship with God grows, our commitment to fulfill the Covenant deepens. A religious person understands that there is nothing more valuable than inheriting God's kingdom. Yet, there are many roadblocks to our ability to seek first the kingdom. For the rich young ruler in Luke's Gospel, his attachment to possessions proved to be an unhappy barrier to entering heaven. Even when offered the greatest treasure, he was unable to surrender to God's will.

We have seen that it is God's will that we give to the poor. Sometimes, a barrier to this commandment is our desire for immediate results so that the impact of our good works will be recognized. Jesus has made it clear that our giving may have a greater impact on our own life than on those who receive our assistance. Some arguments against acts of charity suggest that our giving only perpetuates the problem. But these arguments, which turns us from God to the god of goal fulfillment, are not biblically based.

Within the Christian community, the topic of money has been debated for centuries. Some Christians believe money to be evil in and of itself and interpret Jesus' encounter with the rich young ruler to indicate that all disciples must surrender their possessions. Other Christians view money with less contempt, believing that God only calls us to share a part of what we have.

Whatever view we accept regarding the right use of money, the New Testament affirms that our resources and our talents for accumulating resources come to us as gifts from God. We do not own what we have. We are stewards entrusted with the task of using what is given to us in a responsible way. Likewise, we do not own our children but we are caretakers of lives that belong to God.

The struggle for the rich young ruler was in accepting this wisdom. He could not part with his material wealth because he felt that it belonged to him rather than to God, who asked that he give it to the poor. It is true that Jesus asked for the ultimate commitment as a test. The young ruler, on the other hand, sought a serious challenge by asking what more he needed to do beyond obeying the letter of the law. Jesus urged him to deepen his commitment to God just as Christ invites us to a more complete understanding of discipleship.

If we accept that God is the Creator of all life and Ruler over all that the earth contains, we should not be surprised that God requires us to share what we have. The question facing us is what response we will make when we are asked to increase our commitment of resources to God's Kingdom.

The passage from 1 John 3:17–20 comes from a long discourse concerning life as the children of God. 1 John has much to say regarding love. The passages cited draw the distinction between words and action.

Love is defined as a natural consequence of believing in Christ. Turning one's back on a neighbor in need is not possible for a person who responds positively to God's love. Just as God does not ignore our needs, so we, too, must reach out helpfully to others.

In our world, homeless people can be found in virtually every community. From wealthy areas like Santa Barbara, California and Oak Brook, Illinois to inner cities like Philadelphia and Miami and to the rural farmlands of Iowa, the homeless will be found. When we as the Church see them, how can the love of God be in us if we close our hearts and hang on to our resources?

The biblical perspective teaches us that believers always seek to insure that the basic needs of all our sisters and brothers are met. We cannot allow persons to sleep on the streets while we slowly consider the best approach to help them. We must make the necessary changes in our social structures so that everyone has food, clothing, and shelter. Our reward is great, for it is in giving that we are fulfilled as heirs in Covenant with God who live to enjoy the riches of God's kingdom.

Dorothy's Story

Dorothy was abandoned by her family at a very young age. After two years in an orphanage, Dorothy was placed in a foster-care family. During the next fifteen years, Dorothy had six different foster-care placements. She was a quiet child with learning difficulties who was socially retarded as well. She did not learn to play well with others and, thus, did not develop any friendships.

In high school, Dorothy developed a severe case of depression and was diagnosed as manic-depressive. At age 21, Dorothy was committed to a state mental institution for depression. She learned to like the institutional routine. For the first time, she made real friends. She was liked by both staff and other patients. This was her home for fifteen years.

A variety of new medical treatments for depression were given to Dorothy. Several of them worked well for a few weeks until her symptoms returned. One medication, though, seemed to work better than the others and its dosage was increased steadily. Dorothy changed to become very self-sufficient. After a full year of stable treatment, her doctor pronounced Dorothy cured. The doctor informed her of a new law that made it possible for patients to request release from the institution. Her doctor expressed confidence that if the medicine were taken regularly, she could remain healthy.

Dorothy understood this to mean that she had to leave the institution and she signed the consent forms. She was released with no money and only a 30-day supply of her medication. The last instructions given to her were to have the medication refilled when it ran out.

Dorothy walked proudly out of the institution. She was confident that things would go well. I'll get a job, she told herself, and she walked the streets looking for help-wanted signs.

As night approached, Dorothy became more and more frightened. Suddenly, three young men approached here, knocking her down. They rifled her purse and found her medication. "We can sell these," they said, and ran off with Dorothy's only security. Because she had been institutionalized for so long and given no instruction on her release, Dorothy had no idea how to get more medication. And the muggers had also taken her prescription.

Dorothy spent that first night alone on a park bench. Her understanding was that she could never return to the mental institution after signing the consent forms. Within two weeks, Dorothy was raped three times. Haggard and weary, she can be found now walking the streets. Persons who talk with her find her withdrawn. She causes no trouble at the overnight shelter found for her by the police, nor at the soup kitchen where she eats twice each day. For the most part, she is left alone.

Discussion Questions

1. What does Dorothy need?
2. What would you be willing to do for her? Where in your community would you refer her?
3. What are the physical and mental risks faced by the homeless?
4. Should federal, state and local governments aid the homeless? What responsibility does society have for the poor?
5. In what ways can our churches help? How can churches and government work together?

Additional Texts: Daniel 4:27; Micah 6:6–8; Luke 6:36–38; 14:12–14

Dreams and Visions 6

The status of the religious community is determined by the well-being of its youth.

Purpose: To examine the critical problem of youth homelessness and to promote the need to protect and build up the lives of young people.

Joel 2:28-29; 3:1-3; Acts 2:16-21; Psalms 73; 1 Corinthians 12:12-30

In both the Old and New Testaments, the importance of youth is emphasized. Peter, at Pentecost, quotes directly from Joel's prophesy of the coming era when he says, "Your sons and daughters shall prophesy..." This prophetic vision sees the importance of youth as the future generations who will continue the community of God's people.

In nearly all cultures, youth are seen as a sign for new hope. Joel and Peter use this message to affirm youth as persons worth listening to, both for their words of wisdom and as the hope for the future.

Notice how quickly this image changes in Joel when he lists the evil that has befallen God's people. In chapter 3, Joel informs us that boys were sold for prostitution and girls were exchanged for wine. The younger generation has been terribly maltreated. Joel provides a startling contrast between what has happened and what ought to be the environment in which youth are nurtured.

Joel's vision calls for a community that is secure enough for young men and women to be freed to see visions, to dream, and to hope. Joel further reminds us that these young men and women are our sons and daughters. There is a familial relationship among all persons regardless of their ages.

It is a shocking reality today that so many of our homeless youth quickly become trapped by drug peddlers and pimps. In Joel's day, these crimes occurred because Israel had been invaded by a foreign power and its self-rule was denied. In our day, homeless youth and runaways are preyed upon due to our ignorance and lack of concern.

Every day a stream of teenagers pour into most U.S. cities by way of mass transit or hitch-hiking. They arrive looking for adventure and freedom. They are found quickly by pimps, pornographers, and pedophiles. Even in communities in which social workers are on the lookout for runaways in bus and train terminals, pimps and drug dealers easily attract youth because they can provide money, flashy clothes, and easy access to drugs.

Not all young people are runaways. Some of them are abandoned by their parents, while others are ordered to leave because their families cannot accept them as they are. For example, many youth are asked to leave home when they tell a parent that they think that they might be homosexual. Once they are out on their own, the prostitution trade will gladly put them to work.

When our young persons are treated this way, it is little wonder that many of them have lost hope. The conditions which surround them and the aspirations which motivate our youth will shape our society's dream. Youth are a symbol of a society's energy and vitality. When that is stifled, the people shall perish.

The struggle to maintain hope affects us all. For many of us, the problems of the world appear so heavy that despair cannot be avoided. Persons, committing their time and resources to make the world better, all too often feel cheated by changes occurring too slowly or not at all.

The writer of Psalm 73 shares these feelings. Verses 2–9 describe the utter frustration of seeing the evil doers of the world living so comfortably. The presence of evil has puzzled humankind since the beginning of time. The apparent success of evil draws person toward idolatry and blasphemy. But Psalm 73, like God's work, does not end in despair. God remains the final Judge over all the earth. Our despair teaches us more about ourselves than it does about God. In the final analysis, there is no shelter, no love, no joy without God.

The temptation to surrender to despair assumes that what we now see is all that we will ever see. This view of the world is locked into the moment. When we abandon hope because all that we can see is evil, we allow ourselves to forget that God delivers us from evil. In Psalm 73 and in Joel, although we see evil recognized, it is not as the final authority.

Psalm 73 reminds us that faith in God is a slippery course. At times we will stumble and fall. The lure of false prophets and attractive theologies will beckon us. We need to remember our own temptations when we consider the plight of young persons who fall into manipulative hands. We ought to avoid blaming these victims while working to remove the source of their afflictions.

A continuous source of our despair and anger comes from the belief that we must solve the problems that we see. In response to homelessness, if I imagine that it is my personal responsibility to make everything better, I will be sorely disappointed. Paul reminds all Christians that they belong to the Body of Christ. We are not the Body itself but components of it.

In 1 Corinthians 12:4-11, Paul affirms the unique and special talents that each of us possess. We all have an important role to play which, when joined with others, is capable of producing dramatic results. Our task as Christians is to recognize what our skills are and to offer these freely in unified actions with other persons. In this spirit, the Church will be empowered to promote the Kingdom of God.

Attitudes of despair or frustration at ineffectiveness only weaken the Body. As Paul so aptly summarizes, "There are three things that last: faith, hope, and love; and the greatest of these is love." (1 Cor. 13:13)

The image of the Body of Christ is a reminder that we are not alone. Perhaps the single greatest tool in defeating despair is fellowship with others who share our concerns and burdens. Each of us needs the support of God and the love of others.

Brenda's Story

Brenda grew up in a comfortable suburban community in California. During her teen years, she grew increasingly distant from her mother. She complained to her friends that her mother refused to recognize her maturity. Brenda and her father had never been close. She liked her dad but seldom spent time with him. In order to support the family's suburban lifestyle, the father was away from the home 12-14 hours every day and frequently worked on Saturdays as well. When he was home, he was often tired and irritable.

One day, Brenda and her mother had a terrible argument over Brenda's choice of friends. Her mother was especially concerned about Cindy, a new girl in the neighborhood. Brenda decided that it was time to demonstrate just how mature she really was.

The girls agreed that they would go on a bus trip to Seattle. Their plan was to be gone for a few days to get away from the protective restrictions of their parents. Brenda had her own savings account and was able easily to withdraw $250.00. The adventure of this secret trip was exciting to them and strengthened their friendship. At 4:00 p.m. on Friday afternoon, Brenda and Cindy met at the bus station to board a bus for Seattle. No one else knew about their plans.

Early the next morning when the bus reached Seattle, neither girl had slept well and they were beginning to get scared. Brenda went to the restroom to freshen up. While she was brushing her teeth, someone stole her purse taking all of her money.

Cindy suggested that they go back home but she did not have enough money to purchase two return tickets. As they sat on a bus depot bench, a nicely dressed man approached them and asked if he could help. He appeared to be about the age of Brenda's father and was very kind.

When he learned about their situation, the man offered to let them stay in his apartment for a few days. He said that there was lots of room and the two girls could share a room. Together, Brenda and Cindy felt safe and thought this would be a good option.

The first day went well. The man was gone most of the time. Later that evening, several high school girls came by to visit. They told Brenda and Cindy about the exciting things to do in Seattle. Several of the girls brought liquor. One even offered to share some cocaine with Brenda. Brenda turned the cocaine down but she did have several drinks as the bottles were passed around.

The party lasted late into the evening. Early the next morning, the man told the girls that two business clients of his would be arriving later that day. He explained that the other girls all worked for him as prostitutes or nude models. The nice man was a pimp.

He offered the girls two options. They could work for him and be provided with an apartment and $200.00 per week or they could pay him for the two days that they had stayed with him. His "bill" already amounted to more than Cindy had.

Brenda and Cindy were frightened. They did not know what to do. Brenda was too scared to call her mother for help. Cindy told Brenda that she needed to take a walk, then went to the bus station, bought a ticket, and returned home.

Brenda was left alone with no money. She did not know what to do next.

Discussion Questions

1. When do you feel like Brenda? Have you felt like you had no place to turn?
2. When you study social problems, do you feel despair?
3. How do you cope with it?
4. What spiritual resources are most important in keeping your hope alive? Do these help you in responding to social problems.
5. What agencies exist in your community to help young people? Discuss Brenda's story with your congregation's youth group. What suggestions do they have for Brenda?

Destruction and Rebuilding

7

God calls us to rebuild our decaying communities.

Purpose: To discuss the biblical imagery of destruction with the new vision for renewal.

Ezekiel 16:44–52; 36:8–16; 37:4–14; Nehemiah 2:11–20; 5:1–13; Amos 9:11–15; Mark 13:1–4

Ezekiel, as the other prophets had, scolded his listeners in no uncertain terms for their unfaithfulness. Ezekiel spoke directly both to the people and to the religious leaders. His message began with his pronouncement of an era of destruction, tearing down what had been built. According to Ezekiel, the consequence of turning away from the life-affirming values of God leads to destruction.

The sixteenth chapter of Ezekiel compares the failure of faithfulness to that of sexual immorality. Ezekiel uses shocking images to emphasize the depths of the moral failures he saw. As he announces God's judgement, Ezekiel compares them to the sins of Sodom, using Sodom as the prime example of evil behavior. According to Ezekiel, the sins of Sodom had been pride and a refusal to share food with the poor and the needy. For these transgressions, God destroyed the city.

In biblical history, Sodom serves as the foremost example of Divine Judgement. The ruins of Sodom stand as a reminder of how the God of the Bible differs from other gods. Sodom is an example of God's inability to be reconciled with selfish behavior. The legacy of Sodom is destruction and ruin.

Ezekiel's theme of destruction changes in chapters 36 and 37. Now, the angry prophet visualizes renewal and regeneration. Cities that had been burned would once again be rebuilt and inhabited. The passages cited above are reminiscent of the first chapter in Genesis. After destruction, as once from chaos, creation occurs again, announcing new hope and the birth of future generations.

The image of dry bones coming alive is symbolic of restoration. Ezekiel's vision allows the reader to anticipate building projects and new beginnings. With so many of our cities and rural communities resembling dry bones, Ezekiel's vision encourages us to plan for rehabilitation of buildings and economic structures. Many of our cities yearn for God's life-giving breath.

The symbol of rebuilding urban deterioration assumes narrative form in the book of Nehemiah. Nehemiah tells the story of rebuilding Jerusalem and restoring religious practices. Nehemiah gives a detailed account of the physical rebuilding of the wall around Jerusalem. In Nehemiah we see a destroyed city return to new life.

The fifth chapter of Nehemiah informs us of the poverty facing many of Jerusalem's people. Hunger and the loss of land was prevalent. To improve these conditions, Nehemiah required the cancellation of debts and the return of land to families who had lost this resource.

The content of Nehemiah is more than symbolic. It balances the Sodom image of destruction with rebuilding. For our times, the book of Nehemiah serves as a call to rebuild our communities. For Jerusalem, the rebuilt wall provided protection against foreign armies. Today, our homeless neighbors desire the protection of restored neighborhoods where joblessness and economic changes threaten their security. The Church's task today is to build walls of protection against the crisis of homelessness.

In Brooklyn, New York, the Nehemiah Project has erected the only low-income mass housing there since 1982. Taking its name from the Old Testament story, the Nehemiah Project has built a coalition of church leadership and community organizers to revitalize a neighborhood.

From humble beginnings in 1978, East Brooklyn Churches (EBC) has involved 50 congregations in improving living conditions in a community riddled with crime, drugs and corruption. A first step was to secure a commitment from the Brooklyn Borough president to replace street signs and to begin this project in the poorest areas first. Attention then turned to improving the conditions in food stores. Successes in these campaigns led to the creation of the Nehemiah Project to build affordable housing.

The Nehemiah Project began by raising $7.5 million in church funds which was used to leverage government involvment. New York City agreed to provide tracts of land and to secure interest-free second mortages of $10,000 per housing unit.

In a short time, the Nehemiah Project built more than 1000 two-story row houses at a cost of $53,000 per unit. These are sold to families, many from public housing projects. Purchasers provide a $5000 down payment with monthly mortages averaging $325 to $345. Total purchase price will be $43,000 with a $10,000 second mortgage (interest free) payable to New York City upon resale. The key to the success of this model is home ownership.

The theme of partnership is vital in understanding the model for the Nehemiah Project. Community organizers and congregations joined hands to rebuild a fallen neighborhood. Financial support has come from denominational budgets. Local congregations have provided the organizational base. Community organizers have shared strategies and experience from other cities.

The physical renewal of the neighborhood where the houses stand is obvious. Community stability has also helped the churches. Church growth and community development have worked hand in hand. For example, 11 Roman Catholic parishes in Brooklyn involved with E.B.C. were dependent upon financial support from their Diocese. In seeking support from their bishop these parishes pledged to become self-supporting. After five years only one has not reached this goal.

The goal of urban renewal requires careful planning and attention to economic patterns. A renewed interest by private developers in impoverished neighborhoods has often been a source of homelessness. The influx of private dollars into neighborhoods has generated higher rents and the transformation of low-income neighborhoods into high rent districts.

Economic growth often works against the interests of the very poor by reducing the housing stock. The process of gentrificiation frequently converts multiple family dwelling units into a few apartments. This trend reduces the overall number of rental units. Private developers also change the rental base of a neighborhood by charging higher rents.

Let us look at two recent developments to better understand this problem. In many urban areas, private developers have found inexpensive dwellings to purchase and to rehab. Rising restoration costs force rents to rise well above the previous levels. Private developers will want to get a return back from the investment. Development will seek renters able to afford higher rents. These new tenants will come from different income backgrounds when compared to the previous inhabitants and this will work to change entire neighborhoods. The former tenants will be forced to relocate to other areas.

The crisis of homelessness of the 1980s has shown that as this pattern is replicated without new low-income replacement housing being built, homelessness has increased. The scarcity of low-income housing has only served to drive up the rents for those that remain.

In suburban areas, a similar trend is occurring. The decision by many manufacturing and business offices to move their headquarters to the suburbs has resulted in significant growth for these areas. One of the fastest growing areas of the U.S. is DuPage County—an area that is ranked the tenth wealthiest county in the U.S. with a median family income of $27,509. Yet, a shelter system among churches has been established to serve the area's growing homeless population.

As DuPage County has attracted businesses, the percentage of its population with high paying jobs grows. These persons are interested in and able to afford better (and more expensive) housing. Given normal market reactions, housing costs for the area increased significantly, creating problems for persons on fixed or low-incomes. What was good for DuPage County had a negative impact on the financially less secure.

The dilemma for DuPage County is that its growth has produced a surge in service industries and employment opportunties. However, these jobs normally pay minimum wage salaries and it is difficult to live in the community at that level of earning. DuPage County has a surplus of jobs because people willing to accept those jobs cannot afford to live there. Public transportation access makes it very difficult to live elsewhere and commute. Thus, a boom economy has indirectly led to housing costs related to homelessness.

In returning to our biblical theme, we see that God's People have experienced times of devastation and times of re-creation. This history is evident in our era. When Nehemiah heard the complaints of part of the Jewish community, he acted compassionately.

The era of Nehemiah rebuilt the fallen Temple which was destroyed again shortly after Jesus' crucifixion. Jesus predicted this event in the same tradition of the prophetic announcements of pending destruction.

The image of destruction in the Bible is often interpreted as inflicting human suffering. While God of the Bible takes decisive action, God is not vindictive. Scripture views destruction as a consequence of human sinfulness and as the result of the human community's failure to live as an interdependent family under God. Destruction is not a permanent condition.

When Jesus prophesized the destruction of the Temple, he did not intend to destroy the religious movement he had set in motion. This destruction announced the beginning of a time of disorder out of which God would rebuild and restore. God's Word can be heard in the midst of and in spite of catastrophic events. Evidence of destruction is always a call to return to a life guided by a vision of community life as God's One People.

Human suffering results when we live apart from or in hostility to one another. Christ does not call us to wallow in our fallenness. We are called, rather, to live as restored people who do God's will. God's message to us requires two primary commitments from us. First, we are to love God with all our heart, all of our soul, with all of our strength and all of our mind. Secondly, we are to love our neighbors as we love ourselves. (Luke 10:25-28).

As these words take root in our lives, the dream of our communities resembling the vision of Amos 9:11-15 will become a reality "on earth as it is in heaven." It is to this earthly reality that we are called.

David's Story

David was never particularly fond of school. As a teenager, he was frequently in trouble. His grades were good enough to pass him through school, but David was definitely not college material.

David graduated from high school in 1966. When he got a call from an army recruiter, he decided the army life might suit him. He only faintly recalled hearing Vietnam talked about in school. His parents never watched the news.

Five months after joining the Army, David found himself on a plane to Vietnam. It was the first time he had been more than 300 miles from home. He had no idea what the war was about nor why he was there.

David was assigned to a unit whose job was to perform search and destroy missions. Normally, this meant they walked from village to village seeking weapons and communist sympathizers. At least once a month, David's unit was ordered to burn a village, even though they never found any weapons.

David was haunted by the tears of the Vietnamese watching their villages burn. But his worst memory of the war was the day he was ordered to set fire to a hut, only to learn that a sick woman was unable to escape. Her cries for help left him weak. Many of the soldiers turned to drugs and alcohol to cope with memories like these. So did David.

Many months went by and before David realized it, his enlistment was over. Under no circumstances would he re-enlist. One day, David was helping to burn a village, the next day, his plane landed in Oakland, California.

David began to move from city to city. He readily found jobs, usually washing dishes. He found he liked being alone. He lost many jobs because of his drinking. Others he simply got bored with and left.

David was able to go many weeks without drinking. But whenever he drank a few beers, the awful memory of Vietnam returned. He remembered the smell of burning huts and the cries of sobbing people. These memories always pushed David into a three to four day drinking binge.

David found jobs harder and harder to come by. He began eating in a soup kitchen and learned about a shelter there.

The shelter let David stay as long as he was not drunk. If he was drunk, David slept under a bridge. He was badly beaten there once by a gang of teenagers.

To David, his life felt empty and incomplete. He was often sad. He only talked about his war experience when he was drunk, and when he was drunk, no one wanted to listen to him. The more lonely he was, the more he drank. The more he drank, the more lonely he became.

Discussion Questions

1. How would you help David? Do you feel sympathetic toward him?
2. Is housing a problem in your community? What is being done to build low-income housing?
3. Are you willing to study economic problems? If not, why?
4. If Jesus met David, what would he do?

Additional tests: Lamentations (especially chapters 1, 3 and 5); Isaiah 24:1–18; 41:17–20; 43:1–7

Joy and Celebration

8

We meet God when we share with the homeless.

Purpose: To experience sharing with persons who are homeless as more than mere religious obligation. To show there are rewards for a person who shares which opens up one to knowing God more fully.

Psalm 41:1-3; Jeremiah 22:13-17; Luke 7:19-23; Matthew 25:31-46

Happy is the person who cares for the poor and the weak. The text from Psalms tells us that God will protect and provide us comfort in our times of trial. The person who cares for the poor will be blessed because they will be responding to God's Covenant which binds both humanity and God to reciprocal actions. The Covenant makes clear that if we fulfill our obligation, including providing assistance for the needy, then God will be with us. Persons who help the poor are not guaranteed a life free of difficulty, but they are secure in knowing that the living God will be present in their lives, and this God will answer them when they cry out in either joy or sadness.

Doom upon the person who builds a house on anything but integrity. Jeremiah offers us the consequences of ignoring the case of the poor and the needy. Jeremiah appeals to the people to realize what it means to know God. As we have seen, to know God means to worship Yahweh with all one's heart and mind, to respect God's creation including every person made in God's image, and to build a society where the needs of the poor are met. To live in ignorance or rejection of these tenets is to worship a god other than the true God revealed to us in the Bible. Jeremiah and the prophets tell us that knowledge of God is an active response within a caring community.

The story of the emissaries of John the Baptist visiting Jesus raises the issue of how we know when someone speaks for God. John the Baptist sought God's anointed messenger and directly went to Jesus with the question. Jesus' response was not a direct answer but pointed to the events which reveal to us God's rule. Jesus' answer was not to say, "Yes, I am here," but to provide examples of what happens when God is active in the world. Jesus' answer provides a description of the work of the Messiah—a Messiah who will not command great armies, but who will bring Good News to the poor, and oversee a lifting of their burdens. These are the works of a true leader aligned with Yahweh, and they provide guidance to us in determining how best to serve God in our day.

In the multitude of religious options and debates about Doctrinal Truth, we can still find the People of God in the works of healing and mercy. Matthew 25:31–46 states a startling conclusion about how our actions will be judged. We learn that Jesus is not merely concerned about the poor, but Jesus completely identifies with them. What we do or fail to do about persons who are hungry, homeless, and in prison we do to Jesus. We see in this passage that both nations and persons will be under judgement for their behavior in light of the suffering of persons around them. This passage removes the veil of ignorance as an excuse, for we learn that if we fail to seek and help others, we will have failed Jesus.

Jesus provides us with no exceptions. There is no middle ground, nor is there any mention of the deserving poor nor of the unfairly imprisoned. In fact, the text specifically includes those who are most lowly as well as persons least likely to be considered worthy by human standards. For it is through meeting and helping *even the least of these,* that we encounter Jesus. The person who helps others, finds joy; and the person who fails to recognize this avenue for meeting God, finds alienation.

The last few days of Jesus' life were a time when he demonstrated the strength of his humanity. The Passion Story is appropriately named in that we see Jesus' deeply felt human emotions. In the Gospel accounts of Jesus' last week, we see Jesus weeping with compassion over Jerusalem. Jesus is angry at the violation of the Temple as he throws out the money changers. Jesus experiences the pain of betrayal as Judas participates in the evil of those who want Jesus silenced. In the Garden of Gethsemane, we see Jesus struggling over his own indecision in accepting God's will. Finally, Jesus experiences the pain of the injustice of his sentence to hang on the cross where he is brutally treated by those who publically mock him.

Because we see Jesus experiencing these emotions, we know that the God we follow understands our feelings. As the Church, we can share the story of Jesus' passion with those who also experience anger, betrayal, indecision, and those who suffer injustice at the hands of a world willing to persecute the Prince of Peace. We are called to compassion and to shed tears over our cities who have turned a deaf ear to the words of the prophets and who fail to understand the things that make for peace. We are called to these things because Jesus Christ has entered human history.

We have seen from these texts that the Covenant requirement is more than an obligation to be seen as a duty. We do not need to ritualize sharing with others, because these are not static actions. Each time we help someone, we participate in God's compassion and we experience the joy in being in communion with the Living God of Abraham and Sarah, Jacob and Rachel.

We should also keep in mind that the homeless often bring gifts for us—gifts that are easy to perceive when one takes the time to receive them. The homeless provide more than a way for us to become the People of God. In addition, the homeless give us examples of how a strong faith in God can sustain persons through trials and suffering. It is no surprise to find among homeless persons those who have a strong faith in God. For many of the homeless, God is all they have left. We will also find questions that will challenge our faith and understanding of God. There will be persons who will be difficult to love and our endurance will be tested.

But as People of God, we will come to appreciate that these are the challenges of a full and rich life. We can experience the rich meaning that God has promised us. Through faithful actions, we can bridge the isolation we experience as individuals and become participants in the life created and ordained by God. From this perspective, communion with the homeless offers a way for our faith to be enriched. Following God's commandment to love they neighbor is an invitation to abundant life.

A Volunteer's Experience

Ever since our church opened an overnight emergency shelter, I have volunteered two nights a month. Since there are usually three volunteers each evening, I look forward to talking with the other people with whom I am working and the conversations we are able to have with the street people who sleep in our shelter.

This year when the sign-up sheet was circulated for volunteers, I decided to volunteer for Christmas Eve. This night has always seemed to me to be a significant time for a shelter to be open, since we remember the story of Mary and Joseph not being able to find room at the inn.

I arrived at the church Christmas Eve in a very unhappy mood. My family was angry with me for not being with them on Christmas Eve. Because of some recent problems between us, I was hostile and unfairly critical in my comments. It was not a good holiday experience.

At the shelter, I found that the other volunteers were from our neighboring synagogue. As in past years, our Jewish friends offer to staff the shelter during the Christian holidays. After most of our guests had been provided with a bed for the night, we got to talking. One of the volunteers shared with me the importance of hospitality from the Jewish tradition. She told me the story of Abraham receiving the three visitors in the desert who bring news that Sarah will give birth to a son. We also discussed the significance of Christmas Eve in the Christian tradition and we discovered that our two traditions had many similarities—similarities which led us to work at the shelter.

I was beginning to feel better when a knock came at the back door. Even though it was against shelter rules to let someone in after midnight, I could not bring myself to ignore the knocking on Christmas Eve. When I opened the door a very old, very smelly woman stood before me. Pushing her way into the basement, she demanded a bed for the night. How quickly the words, "There is no room for you here," came to my lips. How angry I became at this unpleasant sight.

But then I looked at the woman again. Her frail, aging face resembled my own grandmother. And then I remembered that we operate this shelter so that people like her do not have to spend the night on the street. I attempted to apologize and direct her to a bed.

She reached in to her pocket and gave me an apple she had saved from a special holiday food distribution earlier that day. "Don't you worry, honey, you are forgiven," she said before lying down.

And I felt it. Forgiveness, not only for how I had treated this woman, but for everything I had done that year that I was ashamed of. And I felt, for the first time, the meaning of God's presence in the poor. This homeless woman brought me the greatest gift I have ever received at Christmas. As the church bells rang from down the street following the midnight Mass, and the shelter guests snored lightly, I knew that God had visited me in the shape of an apple and the life of a beautiful woman.

Discussion Questions

1. Have you ever volunteered in a shelter? Describe your feelings?
2. Can you imagine what volunteering might be like if you have not done this? What concerns might you have?
3. The scripture from Matthew is frequently used. Has it made a difference in your life? What do you think Jesus is telling the disciples?

4. Are their persons you know who are difficult to love? Have these persons helped your life of faith?

Additional Texts: Proverbs 14:31; Psalm 82; Tobit 4:10; Isaiah 1:11-17; Micah 6:6-8; Amos 5:21-24

Changing Priorities 9

The Gospels call us to see the world through the eyes of marginalized persons.

Purpose: To discuss how the insights of the homeless will aid us in examing our own priorities and that of our society.

Luke 14:15–24; Matthew 21:12–17; Psalm 40; Psalm 46; Matthew 14:13–21

This final session begins by looking at a method of teaching frequently used by Jesus. Luke 14:15–24, literally turns the tables on the religious understanding of Jesus' followers. According to the Law of Moses, the excuses given for not attending the banquet were valid. But not to Jesus. Jesus disregards cultural etiquette and reaches out to persons rejected by religious customs. Jesus defines God's realm as open to all. This pronouncement would have been a radical message to its listeners two thousand years ago.

The parable of the Great Banquet has a message of theological urgency and of social reform. During Jesus' lifetime, popular religious tradition interpreted the problems countered by the blind, the poor, the crippled, and the lame as a sign of sin. These persons were seen as bearing the responsibility for a moral infraction that they had committed or one for which a family member was responsible. As a result of this belief, the physically handicapped were denied entry into the holy areas of the Temple and were not permitted to participate fully in the religious life of the community. Jesus defied this logic and proclaimed that these persons, previously banned, were fit for the table. Jesus urged them to enter the banquet and to participate fully in its joy.

In Matthew's Gospel, Jesus took this same action when he threw the money lenders from the Temple. Inside the gates of Jerusalem, Jesus' first action was to go immediately to the Temple and drive the money changers out. His next step was to invite into the Temple the blind and the lame in order to heal them. This was radical behavior. Its impact was not lost on those who began to plot to eliminate this threatening man.

Jesus' unique personality was able to empathize with others and to take bold, decisive action. Just as Jesus had the ability to see the world from another person's point of view, the spirit of Christ continues to call us to the task of looking from the perspective of others.

Many of the Psalms speak clearly to persons who are homeless. The trials and troubles of King David, living in exile, remind many homeless persons of their own difficulties. The Psalms speak of life passionately. They evoke emotions of fear, trust, alienation, anger, joy, and suffering. Study Psalm 40 and 46 as if you were hearing this message as a homeless person. The images of God as a shelter, as a strength, and as a rescuer almost leap off the pages.

For many homeless persons, a popular story from the New Testament is the feeding of the 5000. In each of its versions by Matthew, Mark, Luke, and John, the point is made that there is enough food for all in God's community.

This story shows us the completeness of Jesus' ministry. Jesus is both preacher and provider. His message gave people a new understanding but he also fed their physical needs. It was not enough to provide spiritual food; Jesus also responded to the real need for bread and sustenance.

Theories of economic scarcity are lost in this story precisely because of the actions of the disciples and the crowd. In Matthew's account, night had fallen while the people remained in a lonely place (wilderness). At first, the disciples wanted to send the crowd away so that they could buy food for themselves. Jesus refused to ignore the people's needs, ordering the disciples to distribute what food they had among the crowd. The food was shared until everyone was fed. The food was not fought over nor hoarded. As a result each person had enough (like Israel in its wilderness, fed by manna).

This experience of providing food enough for all speaks to many homeless people of their experiences in soup kitchens. The food may seem repetitious but, at least, in most cases there is enough food. The story of feeding the 5000 reminds operators of soup kitchens, also, of the many times when the crowd outside seemed larger than the food supply, yet when the doors opened every person was fed. Many soup kitchens experience the miraculous joy of an unexpected donation arriving at an opportune time. It is no coincidence that a number of soup kitchens across the U.S. take *Loaves and Fishes* for their name.

A contemporary reading of the "loaves and fishes" story may suggest that it says nothing about economics and the distribution of resources. There are those who would argue that it is unrealistic to claim that adequate resources will be made available in God's Kingdom. This kind of specious argument accepts the premise that economic resources are intended to be in scarce supply.

More accurately, the Bible challenges the way in which resources are distributed in the world. Is it any coincidence that the U.S. has five times the number of billionaires as any other nation while, at the same time, claims the largest population of homeless people when compared with all other western democracies? Consider also how those resources are being spent.

Currently, Congress appropriates over 60 percent of federal tax dollars for military expenditures. In recent years, this has only been possible due to decreases in funding for social programs which were put in place to meet human needs. There is a struggle in the U.S. over the priority of bombs over bread. Bombs are winning.

Many homeless watch this conflict with despair. They feel that they suffer needlessly while the government wastes billions of dollars on military gadgets. They see themselves as victims of war—a war that ignores their needs for housing and employment while military contractors grow richer.

Since the end of the Vietnam War, the U.S. has steadily increased its military appropriations. Many critics of federal housing programs complain that these programs have wasted billions. What these critics fail to mention is that the $300 million spent by the Department of Housing and Urban Development (HUD) from 1970–1986 is less than that which the Pentagon spent in one year, 1987.

In comparing budgets, the discrepancy between what Congress has allocated for housing as opposed to the military budget becomes obvious. Since 1981, the federal housing budget has been cut by more than 75 percent, dropping from $35.7 billion to $14.2 billion in 1987. During the same year (1987), the Pentagon spent five times HUD's budget in the Persian Gulf region alone. Our military commitment to West Germany was twice as large as HUD's entire budget and a military budget category labeled "Miscellaneous Overhead" was $3 billion larger.

As a result of these choices, the low income housing stock in the U.S. has rapidly begun to disappear. According to the U.S. Census Bureau, 14 percent of the U.S. population now lives below the poverty line, an increase of three million people since 1980. Virtually every urban center, the dual trend of rising housing costs and a widening of poverty has caused significant increases in the homeless population. Each year some 2.5 million people are displaced due to evictions, revitalization projects, economic development, and inflation of housing costs. The House Committee on Governmental Operations reports that if this trend continues, the U.S. will inherit a nation-wide housing shortage of 1.7 million units by 1990. The National Reinvestment Corporation in its study, "At Risk of Loss: The Endangered Future of Low Income Rental Housing Resources," predicts that 18.7 million persons may be homeless by 2003.

With these figures in mind and the suffering they point toward, let us remember the kindness of Jesus in distributing the loaves and fishes. Let us also believe in the power that occurs when persons are willing to share with one another.

The Millers' Story

Warren Miller and his wife Jane grew up in a rural farming community in the Midwest during the 1970s. They were married one month after graduating from high school. Warren always had dreamed of owning his own farm and

Jane shared this goal. For seven years, Warren worked as a hired laborer for Jane's father, hoping to be able to save enough money to rent land for the farm he dreamed of buying.

During those seven years of marriage, Warren and Jane's plans to buy land seemed increasingly elusive. First came the couple's three children. The family could not even afford health coverage and they used their savings to pay hospital expenses. Escalating land values pushed up rents. Whatever Warren managed to save was never quite enough. His father-in-law could not understand why Warren was not able to manage his finances better, as he had been able to do thirty years earlier.

Tensions grew within the family as well as between Warren and his father-in-law. Each time Warren asked for a higher salary his father-in-law told him to save more money on lunches and on family entertainment. After long, late nights discussions, Warren and Jane decided that they could earn much more money by taking a job in the city. They calculated that after three years, they could save enough money for a down payment on a farm.

In their calculations they missed three points. First, they did not realize how difficult the transition from rural life to the inner city would be for their children. Second, they underestimated the costs of housing and food. Jane was shocked to learn how high apartment rents were even in the worst neighborhoods. No one had told them that it would be necessary to pay a two month security deposit before moving into an apartment. Finally, they did not foresee the deteriorating employment picture.

At the time that Warren and Jane graduated from high school, many of their friends found jobs in city factories or with construction firms. These jobs were no longer available, nor could Warren locate any of his former classmates. The only job he could find was at a paint company hiring replacement workers for its employees out on strike. Each day Warren had to cross a picket line of angry strikers. He was frequently spat upon. He was paid half the wages that the striking workers had received. His pay fed the family and met the rent. School clothes were another matter and it was difficult to afford pens and paper supplies. After four months, the strike was settled. Warren was told not to return to work the next day.

With two small children at home and one in school, both parents could not work. Warren took a job washing dishes at a nearby hotel and was only able to bring home enough money for rent and food for three weeks. The family joined others like them at a soup kitchen eight evenings per month. But this provided one meal a day and nothing for the child to take to school. Only their pride kept them from returning home.

Despite having paid a two month security deposit, the Millers did not have a lease. They rented their apartment on a month to month basis until they were informed that the next month's rent would be $25 higher. Warren's job could not make up this difference and the lines at the soup kitchen were getting longer. The Millers knew that they were already paying the lowest rent in their neighborhood and Jane could find nothing cheaper elsewhere. In desperation, she even inquired at several near-by shelters. There she learned that she and the children could stay for three months but no men were allowed. No shelter in town accepted intact family units.

Warren had heard that work was available in Texas. After letting their security deposit cover the next two months rent, the family packed all they could into their car to begin the 900 mile journey to Texas. They left with $650 in savings from Warren's job and no plans beyond their hopes for work. In Oklahoma, the car broke down. The repair bill totalled $490. Warren and Jane argued about what to do next.

Discussion Questions

1. Does homelessness show that God's grace has failed?
2. How many homeless people live in your community? What programs exist to help them?
3. Is the Millers' story realistic? Why or why not?
4. If you were a homeless person, how would you view the congregation you worship with?
5. What are the most important needs of homeless families?

Appendix A
Causes of Homelessness

The estimates of the numbers of homeless persons in the United States have varied widely. Whether the actual number is 300,000 or 3 million, every report is clear on two facts: the increase in the occurrence of homelessness is real and there is an acute lack of resources to meet the demand for services adequately.

The 1987 U.S. Conference of Mayors Report *The Continuing Growth of Hunger, Homelessness, and Poverty in America's Cities,* looked at 26 cities and found that the demand for shelter had risen by an average of twenty-one percent. The number of person's requesting but unable to find shelter rose at an even higher rate. Thirty-three percent of the homeless population are families, the category of the homeless population growing faster than all others.

The number of working persons unable to find affordable housing is steadily increasing. The average waiting list for subsidized housing is 22 months. 65 percent of the cities in the U.S. Conference of Mayors Report are no longer taking applications for public housing. In 75 percent of the 26 cities surveyed, families were the largest group for whom emergency shelter is lacking. Only one-third of those eligible are being assisted in housing programs.

Two different economic trends are at work in the United States. During the later 1980s, economic recovery has been felt in a majority of urban areas. However, this recovery has not reached the homeless. For the homeless and the hungry, life has grown increasingly less optimistic.

The homeless no longer fit neatly into personality or economic categories. Today's homeless include persons of

every race, sex, age, and family configuration. A listing of the homeless must include:
—Persons who are mentally ill
—The physically handicapped
—Families
—Abused women and their children
—Abused or neglected youth
—Runaway teenagers
—Unemployed adults
—The working poor
—Persons receiving welfare
—Substance abusers
—Victims of fire, accident, or catastrophic illness
—The elderly
—AIDS victims

The diversity of the homeless population necessitates a multifaceted response. Simple answers fail to adequately address the scope of the problem.

The homeless literally are found throughout the United States. During 1987, Kansas City reported the highest increase in persons seeking shelter with 44 percent. Other cities showing significant increases were Philadelphia (40 percent), San Juan, Puerto Rico (35 percent), Providence, Rhode Island (30 percent), and Los Angeles and Seattle at 25 percent. Many farming families experience the need to move in with relatives. A number pack all they can into automobiles and travel crosscountry in search of employment, reminiscent of the families in John Steinbeck's novel, *The Grapes of Wrath.*

Due to the increased media attention given to the problem of homelessness, most communities have overnight emergency beds. But overcrowding remains an urgent problem. The entire city of Miami has only 275 shelter beds. Denver has 950. Chicago provides 2,500 shelter beds in the winter months but it is estimated that 25,000 will be homeless during the year. Oklahoma estimates its homeless population at 45,000 but has few shelter beds.

The primary issue affecting homeless people is the loss of affordable housing. Boston provides an example of national trends. From 1982 to 1984, more than 80 percent of the housing units with monthly rents of less than $300 disappeared, while the number of units renting for more than $600 per month doubled. The National Housing Law Project estimates that 500,000 units of low-income housing are lost each year in the United States. Since 1980, medium rents rose more than 30 percent for households earning less than $3000 per year. More than 6 million households spend 50 percent of their total income for housing.

Increasing housing costs coupled with a changing economy have worked against the struggles of poor families. The Joint Economic Committee of Congress has shown that 50 percent of all jobs created between 1979-1984 paid less than $7000 annually. The U.S. Conference of Mayors Report indicated that 22 percent of the homeless work full or part-time jobs. Given the difficulties of making ends meet, the July 4th, 1985 issue of the New England Journal of Medicine reports that 35 million Americans have no health insurance. 32 million Americans live in poverty.

Scarcity of housing and joblessness are the primary causes of homelessness. These factors frequently fuel other social problems associated with the homeless. It is well documented that economic pressures lead to drug dependency and domestic violence. Lower tax rates and rising budgets lead to the inability of state and local governments to respond creatively to the mentally ill.

The problems facing homeless people are not ones that will require extensive training or new technologies. We already know how to create jobs and build housing. The question before the United States is whether we have the political and economic will to place the needs of homeless people at the top of the list of national priorities. For most of the 1980s, homeless programs have been funded with whatever was left at the end of the budgeting process. That effort will not do if we are to address seriously the causes of homelessness.

Emergency solutions can go beyond the emergency shelter response. For example, in New Jersey, the Homeless Prevention Program has sought to use rental assistance and loans to help families before they became homeless. This program has developed preventative measures to keep families from being evicted onto the streets and is just one example of innovative responses to the homeless problem. Joint ventures of government, religious, and housing advocates have emerged in communities across the United States.

This is just one example of possible steps in helping the homeless. It is obvious that solving the homeless problem will require resources beyond the religious community. But perhaps, the religious community's greatest asset is its moral vision. God's People are being called to use this asset in new and innovative ways.

Appendix B
Worship Resources

Prayers and Responsive Readings

Oh, God,
Creator and Sustainer of all life,
we come to you in prayer,
knowing that our individual prayers are heard,
believing that our corporate prayers have power.

We remember that prayer is also a time
to be encouraged and renewed
as we seek the directing voice of our God.

Hear us now, oh, God,
and lead us in the ways of justice.

         Amen.

God, we know that you
are with us.

You are our friend and
constant companion.

God, stay with us in times
of trouble and treat us well
when others turn away.

      Amen.

God, be with us this day.
Comfort us as a mother comforts her child,
Protect us from injury,
Nourish us with Word and with bread,
Open our hearts,
Guide our steps,
Remind us during this time together
That we need your grace
and we need one another.

                                Amen.

All powerful God, who hates nothing
that you have made,
teach us to see your love for those
who live without shelter.

We pray for all those who are lonely
and for all those without shelter.
We pray for justice.
Lord, hear our prayers.

                                Amen.

All: God is with us, our strength and our salvation.

Leader: God is our refuge and strength
    a very present help in trouble.
        Therefore we will not fear though the earth
            should change,
        though the mountains shake in the heart of the
            sea;
        though its waters roar and foam,
        though the mountains tremble with its tumult.

People: God is with us, our strength and our salvation.

Leader: There is a river whose streams make glad the city
        of God,
        the holy habitation of the Most High.

>   God is in the midst of her, she shall not be moved;
>   God will help her right early.
>   The nations rage, the kingdoms totter;
>   he utters his voice, the earth melts.
> *People:* God is with us, our strength and our salvation.
> *Leader:* Come, behold the works of the Lord,
>   how he has wrought desolations in the earth.
>   He makes wars cease to the end of the earth;
>   he breaks the bow, and shatters the spear,
>   he burns the chariots with fire!
>   "Be still, and know that I am God.
>   I am exalted among the nations, I am exalted in the earth!"
>
>   —Psalm 46

Leader: Christ has brought good news to the poor.
People: Let us be partners in spreading this message.
Leader: Christ has proclaimed liberty to the captives,
People: And Christ has set us free.
Leader: Christ promises sight to the blind.
People: Open our eyes that we might see.
Leader: Christ uplifts the down trodden.
People: Let us look up, then, to proclaim the year of the Lord.

When I was hungry, you gave me food.
When I was thirsty, you gave me drink.
When I was homeless, you opened your door.
When I was naked, you gave me your coat.
When I was weary, you helped me find rest.
When I was lonely, you held my hand.

When I was a stranger, you welcomed me.
When I was afraid, you calmed my fears.
When I was persecuted, you stood by my side.
When I was ignored, you spoke my name.
When I was happy, you shared in my joy.

Whatsoever you do to the least of these, you have done it unto me.

God, be with us in times of trouble.
Grant us shelter against the bitter wind
and the cold hearts of those who persecute us.

Deliver us from evil.
Guide our feet toward solid ground
as we walk on streets with crumbling sidewalks.

Forgive our weaknesses.
In the harshness of experience we stumble.
Teach us to reach for help and to be reachable.

God, be our Light against the darkness
Grant us peace.

Amen.

Yahweh is an everlasting God,
The Creator of the boundaries of the earth.
God does not grow tired or weary,
but provides understanding beyond fathoming.
Yahweh gives strength to the wearied
and sustains the powerless.
Young men may grow tired and weary,
youths may stumble,
but those who hope in Yahweh renew their strength,
they put out wings like eagles.
They run and do not grow weary,
walk and never tire.

—Isaiah 40:28–31

Sermon Outlines

1. Text: Matthew 5:40-42; John 13:1-15

I rejoice that during my lifetime I have learned to know many persons who are homeless. While I do not rejoice that they are homeless, I cannot deny that my life has been enriched by knowing these persons.

I have learned much about faithfulness from the homeless and I adamantly believe that persons who suffer and endure are often able to share great things.

Several years ago I was speaking to a rural congregation about my work with the homeless. I was asked why I did not seek to "convert" them to Christianity. This question assumed that to be homeless meant a failure to know God.

As I tried to respond to this question, I remembered many homeless persons whose deep and abiding faith has been a vivid testimony to me. I remembered a man named John who prayed each day in thankfulness to God and who lived by the assurance, "God does not care how much a person owns. God looks to see how much you have in your heart." I also remembered the numerous conversations with persons who have been "born again" but who continue to struggle with the harsh realities of life without secure shelter.

In Matthew's version of the Sermon on the Mount, we find these words, "Give to anyone who asks, and if any one wants to borrow, do not turn away." I have heard these words all my life but it is only among the homeless where I have truly seen it occur.

Two women sat next to each other in a soup kitchen on a crisp fall evening. One woman complained about not feeling well and wished for a heavier coat. The homeless woman next to her gave to the woman her only coat and gladly said, "Take this, you need it more than I do." Surely, this act of kindness is the enactment of Christ's loving spirit among us.

Such sharing is not easy for most of us. Even if we have several coats in our closets, we don't want to give away our personal belongings. I have been impressed frequently at the willingness among the homeless to share with one another and to share with me. This ability is made possible, I believe, by their awareness that needing is so immediate. One might conclude that living on the constant edge of hunger and homelessness would cause persons to be very possessive. But I have seen the attitude of open-handed sharing far more often.

For many of us, the dilemma of how to answer a person asking for money on the street is difficult. I remember once seeing the pained reaction of a man begging for money when the person a few paces ahead of me stepped aside and snarled. The eyes of the man who was begging met mine and, for an instant, I wondered about my personal safety if I, too, refused to help. His face reflected anger, sadness, and pain.

All I had was a quarter but, as I offered it, the man's face was transformed into one of cheerful appreciation. How quickly he went from hostility to joy. It seemed a simple act but it produced a dramatic, emotional change.

There will be some persons who may scoff at my action. Others will suggest that it is wrong to give to street people because we do not know how the money will be spent. Have we not all heard the accusation that panhandlers will only waste our money on booze or drugs? It is argued, as well, that giving to alcoholics only serves to perpetuate their problems.

I am not certain about the logic of refusing to give to persons who ask. A literal interpretation of Jesus' words would have us share when people ask it of us. I might find the arguments against doing this more appealing if I did not see so many people willing to pay their taxes without questioning how this money is used. Is it not ironic that we can deny a poor person a quarter on the basis that they might buy alcohol with it and, at the same time, we provide thousands upon thousands of dollars to the government so that it can build and use weapons of mass destruction?

When Jesus encouraged the disciples to share, perhaps the message was intended as a reminder that all sharing is a two-way street. We cannot give of ourselves without receiving some measure in return. Whether it is a simple smile or treasures in heaven, an act of sharing is never a single event.

For the Church of the Brethren, the symbolism of feet washing has a powerful role in shaping our view of mission. The symbol of the towel and basin calls us to wash one another's feet and to have our feet washed as well. This concept of sharing enables persons to receive and to give in mutuality.

My experience in working among the homeless has been to receive many blessings in return. Some I call friendship. Others are examples of lived spirituality which challenges or affirms my own. I have been blessed by the lives of many homeless persons and my understanding of God in the world has been more accurately defined.

2. Text: Psalm 139

The 139th Psalm provides us with the wonderful message that God remains with us in times of joy and in times of darkness. God is our ever present companion. It has been stated that true friendship can be defined as the act of remaining with someone when life turns ugly. Psalm 139 tells us that God is our friend.

Learning to live comfortably within troublesome times has served to deepen my life of faith. Comfort comes from knowing that God stands with me in those experiences. Even though the experiences are unpleasant, the security of God's presence is uplifting.

I have been helped to get past my fears of the dark side of my life through working in a soup kitchen. This soup kitchen fed 40–60 persons each day and, like all feeding programs, had a continual need for supplies. Some days, the options were slim; yet, the hungry kept coming. To increase the food supply, this soup kitchen relied upon food gleaned from grocery stores. This was food removed from store shelves which was determined no longer sellable.

In some cases, the grocery stores gave food away. However, some stores threw the food in dumpsters. Because we were desperate for food, I was willing to reclaim this food from the dumpsters.

Let me emphasize that the food taken from the dumpsters was edible and, in most instances, was quality food. It simply had been removed from the store shelves to make room for fresher produce. For example, when a ten pound sack of potatoes has one or two potatoes spoil, the entire bag is thrown away even though over nine pounds are still good. Or if a new shipment of apples, oranges, or bananas arrives at the store before the previous shipment is sold, the new items are shelved while the earlier shipment is discarded.

My days of dumpstering have been a theological lesson for me. The objective of dumpstering is to be willing to step into a collection of trash and search for what is salvageable. This step requires the courage to stir amidst the garbage. For me, this experience provides a religious understanding to which I refer as a "Theology of the Dumpster." Such a theology understands the value of entering an unpleasant place with the conviction that some good can result. The lesson for me is to accept in faith not only what I like about myself but to claim that which I do not like. I believe it is important in our lives of faith to be capable of seeing ourselves as we truly are, blemishes and all. What the dumpster teaches me is that good news can emerge from less than desirable circumstances.

I emphasize this point because I believe it is often denied within our churches. It is hard to discuss our weaknesses because we fear that these admissions will place us outside the fellowship. We are often encouraged to ignore our dark moments. If we share our anxieties or struggles, people will too quickly say, "Don't say that." They want us only to look at the bright side. These comments are really attempts to keep us away from the dumpsters in our lives.

Occasionally, store owners would chase me away from their dumpsters. In fact, I was nearly arrested once when an irate store owner demanded that I leave "his" garbage alone. It is my belief that the church that serves us well will not act in this way but will rather promise to stand with us in times of distress as well as in times of joy.

Seeking to distance ourselves from the dark sides of who we are does not keep us from having dark sides. Hiding and pretending only work to prevent darkness from being exposed to the light.

The writer of Psalm 139 lets us see that God stands with us in light and in darkness. A life of faith can use both experiences for growth and for discipleship.

3. Text: Mark 9:33-40

The topic addressed in Mark's text centers on the question of how to follow Jesus. The disciples were committed to following Jesus, but there is disagreement and misunderstanding even among those closest to Jesus.

In Mark's Gospel, the disciples are seen in disagreement over two basic questions: 1.) What is true discipleship; i.e., who is great in God's eyes? 2.) How do we distinguish between true and false prophets?

Take the question about greatness. In Mark's Gospel, the disciples are frequently shown to be in conflict with Jesus' intentions. Time after time they ask questions which reveal their limited understanding. The disciples are quick to follow Jesus, but not quite so quick to comprehend.

In chapter nine, we find the disciples arguing about their own claims to greatness. This argument brings to mind the arguments among children over whose house is better, or who can run faster. Greatness in these arguments is based on empirical data; that is, that which is finite and discernible.

Jesus' reference to the child underscores the childishness of the disciples' arguments. Greatness in God's world is not a stair step position. Rather, Jesus argues that greatness is determined by our service to others.

Jesus' understanding of service is a key to unlocking the mystery of faith. The small, the weak, the person passed by are to be served. When Jesus wraps his arms around the small child, he tells his disciples that the "little children" of the world belong to God and disciples are entrusted with their care.

Understanding Jesus' message requires acceptance of the relationship between personal faith and concern for others. To become a servant requires the ability to think beyond our own needs. Service necessitates the willingness to see other's needs and to care enough to help.

The disciples' second question was about who has the right to speak in God's name. This question assumes that God's followers must fit a criteria, as if they belonged to a club or organization. The disciples expressed anxiety when they saw persons they did not know act without their stamp of approval, casting out demons in Jesus' name.

Combining Jesus' response to this question with his concept of greatness points to the following: 1.) God is among those who serve others; 2.) Caring for others is never a contradiction of God's intentions; 3.) Service is a central theme of Jesus' ministry; 4.) One can find God's spirit among persons and groups who are caring for the homeless.

In our world of hungry and homeless people, those tenets can guide us in seeking our own role. Followers of Christ have good news to share—good news that affirms the church's responsibility to care for the poor, to work with others in this venture, and to know that Christ is with us as we serve.

4. Text: Exodus 20:1-6; Deuteronomy 10:17-22; Isaiah 58:1-9

From the scriptures cited, I find three important aspects for today's church in addressing the problem of homelessness.

I read Isaiah to mean that service to others is an act of worship. Worship requires an external God and other people. If I am not confronted by the needs of others, my attention is riveted to my own needs which results in self-centeredness. Isaiah's goal was to broaden our focus beyond ourselves.

Isaiah criticized those whose fasting permits them to quarrel and to oppress workers. Isaiah saw more than a ritual that lacked sincerity. In fasting, a person endures a day without eating. This is difficult for many and, under these conditions, a person is likely to be quick to anger. Isaiah sought to call attention to these feelings and relate them to similar feelings of those who remain hungry after the fasting holiday. Reading Isaiah reminds us that true worship includes remembering the needs of others and acting appropriately to relieve these needs.

My second point uses Deuteronomy's call to see ourselves in others. When Deuteronomy reminds Israel to remember its own time of wandering when strangers visit its land, it is to examine the similarity between the current situation of another person or group with its own historical identity.

It is possible to see the homeless in two ways. We can point out our differences or we can emphasize the common traits we share. While it is true that I have never been homeless, there have been times when my view of life was not unlike how many homeless people feel. I can remember living and feeling alienated from other persons. There have been periods of my life when I felt anger at personal circumstances over which I had no control.

Frequently, the attempts to identify our differences serves to illustrate similarities. An example of this for me comes from the reaction of many suburban Christians when they look at the inner city. It is common for people from the suburbs to see only the bottles and refuse that litter urban streets. They wonder why the homeless cannot pick up after themselves as they do around their suburban homes.

I do not deny that litter clutters the streets of the inner cities. But this behavior is not unique to homeless or poor people. For two years I rode a suburban train. Each evening as my fellow passengers and I left the inner city for the suburbs a variety of drinks and food would be consumed. Many passengers passed their time eating and drinking. What happened at the end of the line? All of the bottles, cups, wrappers, and bags were left on the train for someone else to clean up.

Many of these suburban residents would criticize littering on city streets yet they exhibited the same behavior on their trip home. The only difference there on the train is that people are employed to clean up the trash.

My third point is based on the commandment against making God into a graven image. Idolatry violates God because it seeks to represent the living Creator as an object. The Bible speaks frequently against such actions.

The same injunction against graven images applies to God's creation. It is always a violation of human relationships to label a person as if he or she were an object. Terms like hobo, tramp, bag lady, or street person are not descriptive of people. We are asked to see others as God created them and as God sees them.

In summary, the Bible calls us to:
- —respond to the needs of others;
- —learn to see ourselves in others;
- —to respect God's creation without labels and stereotypes.

In response to this call, today's church must:
- —Reclaim God's concern for the weak and the vulnerable;
- —Receive them as sisters and brothers;
- —Serve them in the style of Jesus;
- —Learn to understand others and their plights so that justice can be served.

The following sermons were shared in worship with homeless people at the Olive Branch Mission, Chicago, Illinois.

Psalm 34—Luke 9:46–48

Psalm 34 speaks to us of joy. I have chosen that text because my life has been filled with joy recently. These past days have been good for me and I want to share that joy. But I need to remember that good things in one's life can be just as distracting in our lives of faith as bad experiences can be.

A temptation when things are going badly is to turn away from God and to feel that God has abandoned us. With joy, the temptation is just the opposite. When things go well we tend to forget others. We may be lured into assuming that life will always be good; therefore, we do not need God. Of course this temptation is only an illusion and most of us realize that sooner or later.

I remember the way a good friend of mine often responded when life had gone well for him. He would stay in a shelter I helped to run in Des Moines and usually would stay with us when he was out of work. This depressed him. After a few weeks, he would find a job. When his paycheck came, he was so thrilled that he would often celebrate by getting drunk. Of course, this was a violation of the shelter's rules and more often than not his "celebrating" caused him more trouble then he found in pleasure. Sometimes, his drinking led him to jail and he would lose his job. He, like so many others, did not know how to express his joy in ways that kept his life going well.

The conversation between Jesus and the disciples in Luke about who is the greatest among them must have occurred during a time when things were going well. After all, why would they argue about being the best on a losing team. We can imagine that success of their work led them to argue among themselves about who was most responsible. Of course, in this argument, we can easily see that they forgot God. They forgot that Jesus was with them and that theirs was a cooperative venture with God. When things go well, we are tempted to take credit—much more quickly than we are willing to assume responsibility when things fail.

Jesus tells us that the greatest evidence of our good work is when we serve other people. Jesus continually reminds us that our behavior affects other people and that Jesus did not come just for a few of us. God loves us all.

Jesus' words speak to us whether our lives are happy or sad. The message is that we are loved and, therefore, we are to love others. When we accept these gifts, our lives will be successful in the eyes of God.

Matthew 6:25-34; Mark 12:41-44

Jesus calls us to have trust and to leave anxieties behind. That is a hard message to give to a person who is homeless. It seems contradictory to suggest that they ought not to worry about being alone on the street without a secure place to stay nor a place to eat. I do not believe that Jesus is suggesting that.

What Jesus does want us to understand is that we need to find God in simple acts. There is a difference between someone who praises God for soup kitchen food and a person who does not appreciate this help from others.

So often, I find people expect God to affect their lives in major ways. People with material wealth want to see lightning and to hear thunder when God speaks to them. People who are homeless simply want God to help them get a job or a place to stay. In each case, these wishes are a significant leap from one's present condition.

I believe that God changes our lives. But I do not believe this happens unless we are able to appreciate the simple, small ways that God is present to us. When we are thankful for the simple gifts, we are open to God's presence.

Many people in Jesus' day failed to realize that he was the Messiah because they were expecting someone different. They wanted a King who was flashier and more dramatic. One who would not spend so much time with poor people. But this is not the God of the Bible and people simply missed Jesus' presence among them.

The story of the widow who offers her last penny is an illustration to us that God appreciates small things and is glad for what we have to share. So often, I talk with people who feel that they have nothing to give, even though I can see that they have much to offer.

I was talking to a man on the street recently. He told me why he was willing to get up early and sell newspapers. He saw this as an act of ministry because he wanted to brighten people's days as they walked by. He said that most of the people he saw getting off the suburban train early in the morning seemed tired and depressed. So, his work was not only to sell newspapers but to smile and say a cheerful "good morning" to them.

I do not doubt that his presence brightened the day of countless people. It was a simple thing but it made a difference in their lives. I see this "service with a smile" as an important ministry.

The people whose lives were brightened by my friend probably did not think of his actions as ministry, nor does he.

But I believe that God feels well served by him and his willingness to do what he can to help other people feel appreciated. I believe that Jesus' statement about the widow applies to my friend.

Luke 24:13-35

After Easter, we begin to prepare our hearts for Pentecost acknowledging that Jesus continues to live through the actions of Christian people. Christ was resurrected.

The story of the road to Emmaus highlights the meaning of Christ's continuing ministry to the Church. In this story, two men who were acquainted with Jesus before the crucifixion were joined by him as they walked on a road. Because they believed that Jesus had died, they did not recognize him. As they walked, they talked and still did not recognize him. It was only when Jesus took the bread, blessed it and began to share it that they recognized him. Their eyes were opened as Jesus shared bread with them.

The Emmaus Road story tells of the completeness of Christ's ministry. Jesus not only shared the Word, he provided both words and sustenance—both knowledge and bread. Jesus is not known by only one of these components.

If Christians do nothing but talk exclusively among themselves about God, the rest of the world cannot have their eyes opened. God is understood only as we share our faith with one another.

Appendix C

Suggestions for Congregations

Education
- Learn more about the problem of homelessness. Use local resource people for this Bible Study guide. Study resources can include audiovisuals, speakers, or written information. Local organizations or service providers are extremely helpful.
- Organize a study group using *Helping the Homeless: God's Word in Action*.
- Remember the homeless in your prayer and worship life.
- If there are other congregations in your neighborhood, invite them to join you in studying this problem.
- Find out what organizations exist in your community to help homeless people. Seek to learn the scope of the problem and areas that need attention.
- Use Vacation Bible School or other special times to study this problem.
- Learn more about the causes of homelessness and possible solutions.
- Look for the homeless as you travel, especially in places you might not expect this problem would exist. For example, O'Hare Airport in Chicago and rural communities are places of residence for many homeless people.

Outreach
- Visit organizations in your community who serve the homeless. Learn what their needs are.

- Write letters to your elected officials and urge them to support legislation increasing services for the homeless.
- Volunteer in a shelter or program helping the homeless. Various shelters can use volunteers during daytime hours, evenings, or weekends. Work to match your availability with their needs.
- Rural congregations can grow garden produce for a soup kitchen or shelter. Find out what vegetables are most needed.
- Collect offerings for the Global Food Crisis fund or for a local shelter. Blanket, canned food, or clothing drives can also be helpful. Ask a shelter what they need most. Toiletry items and undergarments are especially needed.
- Plan activities for children in a family shelter.
- Provide professional services such as accounting skills, medical, carpentry, plumbing, legal services.
- Explore ways of helping the mentally ill.
- If there is a single room occupancy hotel near you, consider adopting a room and/or offering subsidized rents for homeless people.
- Join an ecumenical organization working to develop low-income housing.
- Organize a youth work project in conjunction with a shelter.
- Invite homeless people to worship with you.
- Offer foster care homes for homeless youth within your congregation. Make this a congregational project with shared support.

Appendix D

Resources

Audiovisual

Brethren Press, "A Place to Call Home," Global Food Crisis Fund, 1451 Dundee Avenue, Elgin, IL 60120. 20 minute video, ½" VHS. Available for rental or purchase.

National Council of Churches, "No Place Called Home," Ecufilm, 810 12th Avenue S., Nashville, TN 37203.

Organizations

American Public Welfare Association, 1125 15th Street, NW, Washington, DC 20005.

Brethren Press, Church of the Brethren General Board, 1451 Dundee Avenue, Elgin, IL 60120.

Clearinghouse on Homelessness Among Mentally Ill People, 8630 Fenton Street, Silver Spring, MD 20910.

Committee for Dignity and Fairness for the Homeless, 2001 Spring Garden Street, Philadelphia, PA 19130.

Committee for Food and Shelter, Inc., 815 15th Street, NW, Washington, DC 20005.

Community for Creative Nonviolence, 425 Second Street, NW, Washington, DC 20001.

Community Information Exchange (Homeless), 1120 G. Street, NW, Suite 900, Washington, DC 20005.

Community Service Society of New York, 105 E. 22nd Street, New York, NY 10010.

Habitat (United Nations), 2 United Nations Plaza, New York, NY 10017.

Justice for All National Office, 1334 G Street, NW, Washington, DC 20005.

National Coalition for the Homeless, 1439 Rhode Island Avenue, Washington, DC 20005

National Directory of Services for the Homeless Project Future, City of New York, Human Resources Administration, 60 Hudson Street, Room 9112, New York, NY 10013.

National Housing Law Project, 1950 Addison Street, Berkeley, CA 94704.

National Housing Institute, 439 Main Street, Orange, NJ 17050.

National Low-Income Housing Coalition, 1012 14th Street, NW, Suite 1006, Washington, DC 20005.

National Volunteer Clearinghouse for the Homeless, 1310 Emerson Street, NW, Washington, DC 20011.

Public Technology, Inc., 1301 Pennsylvania Avenue, NW, Washington, DC 20004. Has resource entitled, "Caring for the Homeless: Exemplary Programs."

U.S. Catholic Conference, 1312 Massachusetts Avenue, NW, Washington, DC 20005.

United States Conference of Mayors, 1620 Eye Street, NW, Washington, DC 20006.

Women's Institute for Housing and Economic Development, Inc., 179 South Street, Boston, MA 02111.

Bibliography

Baxter, E., and K. Hopper, *Private Lives/Public Spaces.* New York: Community Service Society of New York, 1981.

Bralt, Rachel G., Chester Hartman; and Ann Meyerson, eds., *Critical Perspectives of Housing.* Philadelphia: Temple University Press, 1986.

Community Emergency Shelter Organization and Jewish Council on Urban Affairs, *SRO's: An Endangered Species.* (Chicago: 1985).

CPL Bibliographies, *Homelessness: An Annotated Bibliography #168.* 1313 E. 60th Street, Chicago, IL 60637.

Erickson, Jon, and Charles Wilhelm, eds., *Housing the Homeless.* New Brunswick, NJ: Center for Urban Policy Research, Rutgers University Press, 1986.

Halpern, Joseph, et als., *The Myths of Deinstitutionalization.* Boulder, CO: Westview Press, 1980.

Harrington, Michael, *The New American Poverty*. New York: Penguin Press, 1984.

Hombs, Mary Ellen, and Mitch Snyder, *A Forced March to Nowhere. Homelessness in America*. Washington, DC: Community for Creative Nonviolence, 1982.

Hope, Marjorie, and James Young, *The Faces of Homelessness*. Lexington, MA: Lexington Book/D.C. Heath and Company, 1986.

Hopper, Kim, and Jim Hamberg, *The Making of America's Homeless: From Skid Row to New Poor 1945–1984*. New York: Community Service Society of New York, 1984.

Kozol, Jonathan, *Rachel and Her Children*. New York: Crown Books, 1988.

National Coalition for the Homeless, "Stemming the Tide of Displacement: Housing Policies for Preventing Homelessness," September, 1986.

Rousseau, Ann Marie, *Shopping Bag Ladies: Homeless Women Speak About Their Lives*. New York: Pilgrim Press, 1982.

Salverno, D., K. Hopper, E. Baxter, *Hardship in the Heartland: Homelessness in Eight American Cities*. New York: Community Service Society of New York, 1985.

Sexton, Patricia, *Homelessness. A Selected Bibliography*. New York: New York University Press, 1982.

Epilogue

I began this Bible study by thinking about my work with the homeless which began seven years ago. Those years have led me to strengthen my personal commitment in anticipation of the years ahead. It will be necessary for the issue of homelessness to remain an active concern. It is my intention to commit myself to keep before me the plight of homelessness in the years to come.

That commitment is only possible because of the following reasons:

1. The love and support of my family who share that love not only with me but with the homeless.

2. The ability to pray and to renew energy from spiritual resources. The anguish and the joy of my work have taught me to pray in ways that affirm my own needs while remembering God's love for all persons.

3. The relationships I have enjoyed with homeless people. I consider many of these persons to be friends and I have benefited greatly from knowing them.

4. Finally, I have been deeply touched and supported by the commitment of other persons and the willingness of the Church to respond to this pressing problem. Homelessness is an area where God's people frequently join hands in mutual work.

I am frequently asked how it is possible to keep hope alive in a world of increasing pain and suffering. I can only respond by pointing to the growth of my own skills in coping with disappointment and frustration. These are skills which I have sharpened primarily through working with homeless people. I have vivid memories of persons whose lives have contained nothing but pain, yet who are still able to reflect God's love is a source of great encouragement for me.

During the week that I was working on the final draft of this resource, I was asked to moderate a discussion between a neighborhood organization and a church that planned to open a shelter for 18-20 year old males. It was quickly apparent that this would be an unfriendly meeting. Two opposing goals emerged: 1) the church's commitment to serve others, and 2) the organization's fear that their property values would be adversely affected. In simple terms, this was a classic struggle between a concern for persons against a love of property.

Seven years ago, I doubt that I could have been able to moderate such an exchange. My emotions would have been totally with the chuch and I would have been hostile to any opposing view. Even though I still sided emotionally and theologically with the church's position, I could understand the argument of the persons on the other side better than I might have a few years ago.

Rather than simply seeing these people as wrong, I began to recognize in them the same characteristics I see in the homeless. They, too, were motivated by fear, alienation, and a lack of knowledge. They had trouble reaching out to others because they did not feel that others cared about them. They were threatened and angry.

As I saw in them traits I see in the homeless, it was possible to feel compassion and understanding. It is my hypothesis that these reactions will be useful in helping all people overcome their fears and anger.

My fundamental belief that Christians must embrace a theology that acknowledges the power of love as predominate remains. Even as we experience hatred and prejudice, we must remember that our love can call the world toward truth and understanding in the same way that God is calling us toward reconciliation.

I do not use these words without knowing that writing them is far easier then living them. Faithful living must experience grace as well.

My faith is strengthened when I remember the work of Paul and the first Christians. The early years of the Church were hardly pleasant ones. Those disciples faced hostility, misrepresentations, rejections, homelessness, sinful behavior, and internal dissension. Yet, God provided them with the resources to go on and to remain obedient. Two thousand years later, God offers us the same assistance.

Let us go forth then to love and serve the God of Abraham, Sarah, Jacob, Ruth, Isaiah, Peter, Paul, the homeless and the housed. Let us go forth to love and serve the God who gives us life.

Christian Social Involvement
1990

Duane Grady

" HELPING THE HOMELESS"

DATE DUE			

Get with it!
Get Response!